Teacher Talk

Studies in the
Postmodern Theory of Education

Joe L. Kincheloe and Shirley R. Steinberg
General Editors

Vol. 123

PETER LANG
New York • Washington, D.C./Baltimore • Boston • Bern
Frankfurt am Main • Berlin • Brussels • Vienna • Oxford

Raymond A. Horn, Jr.

Teacher Talk

A Post-Formal Inquiry into Educational Change

PETER LANG
New York • Washington, D.C./Baltimore • Boston • Bern
Frankfurt am Main • Berlin • Brussels • Vienna • Oxford

Library of Congress Cataloging-in-Publication Data

Horn, Raymond A.
Teacher talk: a post-formal inquiry into educational change / Raymond A. Horn, Jr.
p. cm. — (Counterpoints; vol. 123)
Includes bibliographical references (p.   ) and index.
1. Educational change—United States. 2. Postmodernism and education—United States.
3. School improvement programs—United States. 4. Teachers—United States. 5. Teachers—Training of—United States. 6. Education—Research—United States—Methodology.
I. Title. II. Series: Counterpoints (New York, N.Y.); vol. 123.
LA210.H674   370'.973—dc21   99-15922
ISBN 0-8204-4558-4
ISSN 1058-1634

Die Deutsche Bibliothek-CIP-Einheitsaufnahme

Horn, Raymond A.:
Teacher talk: a post-formal inquiry into educational change / Raymond A. Horn, Jr.
—New York; Washington, D.C./Baltimore; Boston; Bern;
Frankfurt am Main; Berlin; Brussels; Vienna; Oxford: Lang.
(Counterpoints; Vol. 123)
ISBN 0-8204-4558-4

Cover design by Lisa Dillon
Cover art by Nancy Anderson

© 2000 Peter Lang Publishing, Inc., New York

All rights reserved.
Reprint or reproduction, even partially, in all forms such as microfilm,
xerography, microfiche, microcard, and offset strictly prohibited.

Dedication

Teacher Talk is dedicated to Ray and Jane Horn, Bill and Mary Jane Hawk, Ed and Edie Zehring, Ray and Mildred Burkhart, Herman and Grace Royer, Peggy and Abram Buffenmeyer, Paul and Betty Gensemer, and to the rest of the greatest generation who did what they had to do.

Table of Contents

Preface	ix
Introduction	1
Chapter One The Failure of Educational Change	9
Chapter Two A Post-Formal Inquiry	21
Chapter Three Education in Crisis: The Postmodern Context	43
Chapter Four A New Direction	69
Chapter Five Teacher Talk: Post-Formal Stories	111
References	161
Appendix A	171
Appendix B	173
Appendix C	177
Appendix D	181
Appendix E	183
Index	185

Preface

Thirty years is a long time for any job; however, any teacher will tell you that there are weeks, semesters, or years that seem like an eternity. Often this temporal phenomenon is assumed to be an inherent aspect of the profession. This phenomenon is often seen as a manifestation of a variety of factors including, but not limited to, the type of students, the career stage of the teacher, personal problems, change in administrative style, or merely, in some cases, boredom from the repetitiousness of teaching the same old thing. Another more enervating factor is the professional isolation in which most teachers work. Creativity is dampened, challenges are not raised, and critical introspection of one's work is hard when one is isolated. Only a teacher understands this pervasive isolation. Only teachers understand that traditional faculty meetings, lunchroom chatter, and occasional hallway conversation are not enough to offset the deleterious effects of their professional isolation.

What teachers do not understand is that the isolation is also a political tool whose effective controlling power keeps them in line, socially, curricularly, and politically. It is a tool wielded by those whose contradictory purposes of facilitating teacher creativity and motivational energy and at the same time keeping tight control over teachers result in the paper changes that satisfy audits and mandates but not the parents, students, teachers, administrators, and business people who so vociferously criticize the effectiveness of education. In addition, the emotional consequences of professional isolation play themselves out in a number of ways, ranging from professional esteem issues to unrealistic and negative opinions of other faculty that rupture relationships and blunt the projects and initiatives of other faculty members.

Teacher Talk is my attempt to explore methods and ideas that can ameliorate the deleterious effects of teacher isolation. The structure and organization of schools will undoubtedly not change, especially since the search for answers to the criticisms of public education is in the direction of standards (for teachers and administrators as well as students), vouchers, and mandatory professional development. I doubt anyone will seriously look back to the open classrooms staffed by interdisciplinary teams.

The overriding premise of this book is that substantive educational change cannot occur without conversation. Not the kind of conversation that currently is ubiquitous in our schools, but a post-formal conversation that facilitates new educational designs, creative problem solving, and personal and collective critical reflection on theory and practice. The most important attribute of post-formal conversation, in facilitating change, is its ability to empower those who participate in it. However, power is linked to knowledge, and to increase their power teachers need to increase their knowledge. Unfortunately, increasing teacher knowledge is most often construed as increasing teachers' knowledge of subject matter and instructional methodology. What needs to be increased is the knowledge gained through the process of critical reflection on their past experience—experiential knowledge that includes relationships, visions, emotions, and self-esteem. Critical reflection on the past informs the present and creates possibilities for the future.

Connelly and Clandinin (1999) write about "teachers as knowers of learning" (p. 1). To understand teacher knowledge, they coined the phrase "personal practical knowledge" which is:

> a term designed to capture the idea of experience in a way that allows us to talk about teachers as knowledgeable and knowing persons. Personal practical knowledge is in the teacher's past experience, in the teacher's present mind and body, and in the future plans and actions. Personal practical knowledge is found in the teacher's practice. It is, for any teacher, a particular way of reconstructing the past and the intentions of the future to deal with the exigencies of a present situation. (Connelly & Clandinin, ed., 1988, p. 25)

However, isolated individual reflection is a necessary but not sufficient condition in the empowering of teachers through the self discovery of their personal practical knowledge. *Teacher Talk* proposes that the attainment of personal practical knowledge is most effective when occurring through the medium of conversation—critical conversation with other professionals.

Through post-formally conversing about unconventional professional development topics such as postmodernism, systems theory, school culture, spirituality, and qualitative research, teachers can uncover new information that will help them critically construct new meanings about their past experience, their current situation, and their future possibilities. Schools are purposefully ahistorical in that aside from sports history, most stakeholders have no idea what went on prior to their arrival and, therefore, cannot use that information in an empowering context. Developing or rediscovering the history of one's institution history, through the many lenses previously identified, is, in itself, an empowering experience.

I want to thank Pat Horn for her support in this endeavor, and for her effort, as a public school board member, in resisting oppression at that level. J. Dan Marshall, Jamie Myers, Alison A. Carr-Chelman, and James Nolan provided invaluable feedback in the development of this project. A special thanks to Joe L. Kincheloe and Shirley R. Steinberg for their mentoring and encouragement through the opportunities they extended to me. Dan Brensinger, Dave Laurus, Sue Means, Barry Mentzer, and Steve Schwilk must be recognized for their inestimable participation. These career teachers deserve special recognition for having fought the good fight in their own way for all those years. As creative as ever, Nancy Anderson contributed the cover art; just as she contributed so creatively to the growth and development of her students. Also, a special thanks to my daughters, Cynthia Jane Horn and Jennifer Maude Horn, whom I could always count on for their unswerving support in difficult situations. Thanks to Michael Szutowicz for his care and friendship and to Richard P. Kluft for his guidance. Finally, special thanks to my editors, Christopher Myers, Bernadette Alfaro and Lisa Dillion, who guided me through this arduous but rewarding process.

Introduction

As a career high school teacher for three decades, I have been constantly immersed in educational change. There always seemed to be a need for change because apparently the status quo never adequately met the needs of the school community. Educational fads would come and go, along with the accompanying educational consultants hawking their wares. Curriculum and instruction always seemed in a state of flux, as change agents quickly moved to the next panacea. My problem is that after all these years, I have the sad sense that things never really did change. As I leave public school teaching, I find my high school as tradition-bound as it was thirty years ago. Students are tracked, teachers direct student activity and transmit knowledge, and students sit in rows. Did all of the reforms fail because of our lack of professional efficacy, or is education, as a social system, truly impervious to any substantial change?

At first the uneasiness about my efficacy as a teacher manifested itself only when a change initiative failed. Then like an insidious disease it reappeared more often, and finally like a rapacious cancer it spread to other aspects of my professional experience. Within a few short years, no areas of my curriculum, instruction, or classroom management strategies were unaffected; in relation to their educational effectiveness, all were suspect. Unease, doubt, and recrimination characterized all of my reflections on my educational experiences. When something failed, the blame had to lie with either those damned administrators, or the undisciplined, unmotivated students, or the poor childrearing practices and poor genetics of the parents.

Explaining this bleak vision requires three disclosures. First, my teaching career started amidst an unbridled sense of optimism that my generation and I could indeed change things for the better. After the initial efforts driven by this unrestrained optimism, and after the realities of life set in, my quest for successful change continued in either frenzied improvisation within my own domain or in a sustained systemwide change initiative in concert with my colleagues. During these efforts at change, I remember concluding that those faculty and administrators who fell short in their commitment to change obviously did not care as deeply as I did about bettering education. Thoughts like this not only exacerbated my unease and doubt about my own efforts but also invariably drove a relational wedge between us.

Second, as my sense of efficacy in the classroom faded, I found the opposite to be true in relation to the extracurricular activities in which I was engaged. The sports, clubs, and student service organizations in which I coached and advised provided unique opportunities for me to make a difference. I noticed that some teachers focused exclusively on their favorite extracurricular activities and did outstanding jobs in building effective organizations in which students flourished, while at the same time they made only a minimal effort in the classroom. Common comments were, "I'm here to coach, not to teach," or "I don't believe that I could come in here [to the school] if it wasn't for the coaching." Whether they were coaching athletes, advising classes and clubs, or producing musical and theatrical presentations, the teachers' positive energy and motivation flowed always from the classroom into the extracurricular activities. Teachers who were pedantic and dismal in the classroom were creatively brilliant, sensitive, and efficient in pursuing their extracurricular goals.

Of course, not all teachers used extracurricular activities as their creative outlet; because of economic necessity (prior to the last fifteen years, teacher reimbursement was lower than in other professions) many teachers worked second jobs. In their evenings, weekends, and summers they would leave the school and go to work elsewhere. Teachers were valued employees, greatly sought after by construction companies, insurance agencies, and real estate agencies. In some cases, these companies actively recruited teachers. Food markets, restaurants, beer distributors, and other retail establishments felt fortunate to have a teacher as a part-time manager. Obviously, we had the skills and work ethic to be successful; why then could we not effect significant change in our chosen field? Why were we valued as realtors, waitresses, and carpenters but not as educators?

Finally, not only was the unease and doubt about my efficacy as an educator exacerbated by the continuous failure of my change efforts and by my personal validation as seen in my success in the outside world of work, but the empathy and compassion that are inherent and ubiquitous in education actually fueled my negative feelings. Caring is a two-edged sword in that while it generates powerful motivation to help others, when the efficacy of that help is denied, it can result in despair and depression. I always had a sense that most if not all of my colleagues truly cared about their effectiveness as educators and thus about the welfare of their students. However, what does one do when merely caring is not enough? Unfortunately, as the years passed I noticed a pervasive conditionality in the faculty's commitment to their profession in general, and specifically to their classroom. Each of us arrived at an accommodation that would maintain our personal esteem and efficacy and would allow us to survive the negativism that permeated our professional lives.

What are the causes and outcomes of such a bleak vision? Both causes and outcomes become intertwined, perpetuating a condition such as this. Burnout, teacher and administration adversality, professional isolation, covert and overt resistance (at first toward the perceived problem-makers, then generalized to everything), disillusionment, and selective accommodation join in a dance of causality.

How then does anything get accomplished? How is it that children learn if many of their teachers are mired in such bleakness? The more germane question is how much better could education be if we can accomplish so much within these constraints? The situation is obviously more complicated than this brief contextualization reveals. The research on teacher career stages provides a more detailed explanation of a thirty-year career than my summary has done. Also, education is a human system that must to some extent achieve its systemic goals. Despite education's well-documented resistance to change, educators must be responsive to the input from the larger societal systems in which education is embedded. Another aspect of education's problematic relationship with the larger social system is that the substantial achievements of education are mostly ignored, or in some cases denigrated, by education's diverse and plentiful detractors.

Valuing Teacher Experience

Teacher Talk is an attempt to broaden our understanding of educational change by focusing on the gatekeepers within our schools, the teachers. Much is written about the role of the teacher in educational change, but seldom are teachers given an opportunity to critically reflect upon their experience. The previously described bleak vision of education is my interpretation of my experience. Undoubtedly, some teachers would immediately concur with most of my interpretation, but I personally know some who would take issue with every aspect of it. Those who would take issue are mostly younger teachers (in terms of teaching experience) who enthusiastically and dutifully transmit factual knowledge on a daily basis. Traditional teaching and assessment characterize their pedagogy. They feel good about their salary and about their professional effort. They work hard, put in long hours, and are less involved in extracurricular activities than other teachers are. They teach as they were taught, with the greatest innovation being the computer, which they use primarily for teacher preparation and in a teacher-directed context within the classroom

From my perspective, I ask why they cannot see the negative aspects of their pedagogy and professional behavior. My first conclusion is that they lack a historical understanding of their profession and their school. A sense of history is a prime prerequisite for critical reflection on experience. Also, these younger teachers lack the opportunity to engage in autobiographical reflection. Remembering and reflecting on remembrances in conjunction with a knowledge of the history of one's profession and school are essential elements in identifying one's place within one's profession and school. However, these teachers lack the opportunity and skill to critically reflect upon their experience. By "critical" reflection I mean reflection on power, and how it is manifested in the relationships between all stakeholders of the educational system in question.

Currently Pennsylvania is in the last year of a two-year early retirement program for teachers with at least 30 years of service. Two commonly held beliefs about the benefits of this program are the boon of a reduced payroll for the school districts and an influx of new ideas that will arrive with the younger teachers. However, one disadvantage is the loss of history and the consequent deleterious effects on teacher culture within the schools with the largest numbers of retirements. Often, teachers have no sense of what has come before in their profession and especially in their school. Of course, one could speculate that a more pragmatic, hegemonically oriented administrator would welcome this lack of history. If teachers are without a historical foundation based on their shared cultural and political history, then an instrumentally disingenuous history can be provided for them and used to control their interpretations about current and future educational initiatives and their own current and past pedagogical efficiency.

Teacher Talk describes a qualitative model that provides an opportunity for critical autobiographical reflection. The teachers who participated in this opportunity were older teachers near the end of their careers;

however, the ideal professional development activity would be to provide such an opportunity for both young and old teachers to share their history and interpretations and to mutually construct meanings about their experience that would build community. Of course, the true ideal would be to have all stakeholders participate, but, this possibility is not consistent with the current reality of our school systems.

The primary purpose of what transpires in *Teacher Talk* is not so much for us to understand the teachers but for them to understand themselves in relation to their experience. For this to occur, the teachers must first remember and then reflect upon their experience. However, change requires more than reflection; it requires professional growth. The qualitative method, as described in *Teacher Talk*, was also a professional development strategy in which relevant, appropriate theory was introduced into the reflective conversation. In this manner, not only were the teachers able to better understand themselves and their experience, but they were also able to broaden their understanding of their experience through their authentic engagement of new educational and systems theory. Therefore, *Teacher Talk* is about both stories and theory. It is about the stories that teachers construct about their experience and the authentic introduction of theory into relevant conversation.

Overview, Audience, and Purpose

The questions and emotions raised by my reflections led to a formal exploration of educational change that resulted in this study. My research proposes that educational change fails on at least three fronts: modernistic professional development strategies are inadequate in the face of postmodern problems; the equitable inclusion of teachers in policy making is a necessary yet unmet condition for successful change; and teachers' construction of their meanings about change is an essential, though routinely ignored, element in understanding teacher attitudes toward the implementation of change. The implication of my proposition is that teachers are central to effective change, and through a post-formal type of professional development they must develop the post-formal skills to deal with the critical issue of power, develop a systemic view of their profession, and build an egalitarian community through post-formal conversation.

Five other career high school teachers and I explored my proposition, through open-ended critical reflection. This method facilitated the examination of our experience with educational change and our subsequent constructions of meaning about this change. The following narrative provides an experiential framework for our shared experience with educational change and discloses my construction of these events. Sue, Barry, and Dan are English teachers who shared these experiences, and Steve, Dave, and I are members of the social studies department. All the participants have taught at this high school for their entire careers. Sue has taught for 29 years, Barry for 31, Dan for 40, Steve for 31, Dave for 29, and I for 30.

Each person's story will continuously unfold throughout the first four chapters. Chapter Five will conclude each story by focusing on a debriefing with each participant and, in addition, will conclude the story of this research method. Interspersed throughout *Teacher Talk* will be the inclusion of theory that is relevant to educational change and the experiences of the participants. Some of the theory will be discussed in detail due to its special relevance to the problem of educational change. My role is that of participant-researcher and will be assessed in relation to the interpretations made by all participants and in relation to the catalytic effect this type of researcher role can produce.

I have written *Teacher Talk* for multiple purposes and diverse groups. I especially hope that *Teacher Talk* can be instructive to teachers and administrators who are engaged in change initiatives and to younger teachers who may lack the more personal history that broadens the context of their professional understanding. Since my research dealt with older career teachers, I feel that it is especially valuable for the younger teacher. The blend of personal reflection, educational theory, systems theory, and postmodern contextualization make *Teacher Talk* an invaluable resource for pre-service teachers and graduate students. Having been an educational consultant I have found that consultants and curriculum developers often lose sight of the teacher-as-person, and therefore they are not able to tap the power of the teacher-as-gatekeeper. In many cases, the consultant or curriculum developer inadvertently alienates the teacher and actually strengthens the teacher's imperviability to change.

The purpose of *Teacher Talk* is not to provide a formula or recipe that will guarantee successful change or the establishment of an egalitarian community. The modernistic assumption that a step-by-step procedure can be generalized to other situations and can consistently lead to successful change is inherently fallacious. The essence of a post-formal inquiry, as proposed in *Teacher Talk*, is the recognition that, first, education, like life, is unpredictable and complex, and, second, an eclectic array of epistemologies and methodologies must be available to navigate this complexity. This essence must be further understood in the context in which teachers construct their own meanings about their experience; and to understand change or to promote change, the change agent must engage the teachers on the level where they reflect on their experience and consequently construct their meaning. Without knowing what the teachers are thinking, change agents cannot assess the teachers' commitment to the change initiative. Therefore, the multiple purposes of *Teacher Talk* include the following:

- an exploration of the epistemologies that teachers must engage to understand all that is related to educational change;
- a review of conversational theory that will lead to more effective stakeholder communication;
- a presentation of a researcher-as-participant qualitative research method that can facilitate critical reflection and dialogic conversation among teachers; and
- the provision of candid teacher talk on a personal level about a lifetime of educational experience.

Chapter One

The Failure of Educational Change

In 1969 I began my career as a social studies teacher in a rural public high school that was curricularly and instructionally traditional in that it was rigidly hierarchical, centralized, and teacher-centered. Larry Cuban's description of teacher-centered instruction summarizes the condition that I found. Instruction was "aimed at imparting knowledge from a text with little evidence of student involvement in critical thinking, problem solving, or experiencing how scientists worked" (1993, pp. 4–5). The "teacher controls what is taught, when, and under what conditions within a classroom" (Cuban, 1993, p. 6). Teacher talk exceeded student talk, instruction more frequently involved the whole class than groups, and classroom furniture was arranged in rows facing a blackboard (Cuban, 1993). However, change was on the horizon. Prior to my employment, a new superintendent was hired, and a former social studies teacher, who had just completed a doctorate, was given the assistant superintendency. These two people began the formulation of a master plan of change that would attempt to radically reconstruct the curriculum and the instruction in this school.

Curriculum and Instruction

In 1969 the call for change was made. The school district's new philosophy of education proposed that the school would become "a place where the individual assumes increasing responsibility for his own actions. Classrooms should be places of inquiry, open discussion, and discovery. The school must assume a role in which they do more than preserve the status quo or exist a mere cut above their immediate surroundings" (Cocalico School District, 1969, p. 10). Specific targets were identified, such as introducing non-gradedness, new concepts in grouping for large- and small-group instruction, and flexible scheduling .The use of newly developed teaching machines and independent study programs, together with the development of conceptual/inquiry learning approaches, was another target. In addition, buildings were to be redesigned, in-service activities increased, communication within the school community improved, and teacher and student involvement in planning educational pursuits expanded.

Coincidentally, the demographics of the school district were changing. Population growth required the employment of many new teachers. All of these were first-year teachers. This influx of young teachers was seen as a benefit of the current "high state of flux" due to "many innovations [that] have left the drawing boards and are now in the experimental stage," thus necessitating "the twin concepts of versatility and flexibility" (Cocalico School District, 1970, pp. 1–2). The assumption was that the young teachers would be more receptive to radical change. The English and social studies teachers who were the subjects of this research, including myself, were among the new teachers who experienced the ensuing change initiatives.

As the years progressed, my colleagues and I encountered many innovations and participated in their attempted implementation. Some were my own individual initiatives, while others were part of a schoolwide or systemwide effort. My first individual venture was in the High School Geography Project (HSGP) (Association of American Geographers, 1970). This National Science Foundation-sponsored program moved instruction from the presentation of teacher-centered textbook geography to a hands-on, high-interest, activity-oriented approach. Maps, simulations, spectroscopes, interviews, critical thinking, individual and small-group work, and local field research were all part of this program.

At the same time, decisions were made to develop mini-courses in the high school that would be offered for student selection based on individual interests. The HSGP offered six different mini-courses for the students, and the associated innovative instructional practices provided the basis for other social studies courses. In 1973, the high school faculty began the development of mini-courses with social studies leading the way. The social studies department initially offered 35 nine-week, quarter-credit courses. In one form or another from 1973 to 1989, the mini-course format comprised the basic structure of the social studies curriculum. The early 1970s were marked by a pervasive optimism characterized by an intuition that what we were doing would make a significantly positive change in the education of our children.

Another aspect of the curricular change was the development of an individualized teamteaching program for twelfth-grade social studies and English. This program, the Introduction to the Social Studies (ITSS), was actually of a parallel disciplinary nature: the two departments did not teach side by side, but each reinforced the other's curriculum. All seniors worked with this team for a two-hour block of time each day. The team had full authority in utilizing this time and structuring the students' activities in any way. Both departments created three 12-week courses in which the English and social studies curriculums would complement each other.

The social studies department created a curriculum motivated by the value of these ideas: teaming with consensual decision making; variety in curriculum, instruction, and assessment; teacher-made or teacher generated materials; student choice; activity-oriented learning; heterogeneous grouping of students; small-group and individualized instruction; individual and group oral testing; and scientific precision in managing and teaching students, as well as in writing objectives and instructions. At appropriate times, students worked on individualized learning packets, played roles in large and small simulations, critiqued audio-visual presentations, worked in small learning groups, completed group and individual projects, experienced traditional assessments, participated in group oral evaluations, and took individual oral tests.

Students frequently critiqued primary sources. In one 12-week course, Introduction to the Humanities, the 1930s provided the basis for study. Within this multimedia course, students participated over a nine-week period in a stock market game that simulated the panic of 1929, read John Steinbeck's *Grapes of Wrath*, read numerous primary source documents, and critiqued radio programs, music of the period, a Busby Berkeley musical, an Errol Flynn movie, a Marx Brothers movie, and the movie *The Grapes of Wrath*. They also studied Franklin Roosevelt's New Deal.

The parallel disciplinary nature of the program, as constituted by the coordination of curriculum between the two departments, only lasted one year; however, the social studies faculty used this experience as the basis for adapting their curriculum to an open-space facility. An emotional and relational outcome of the ITSS program's demise was the tempering of the optimism that had previously characterized our attitudes toward our collective ability to create viable and sustainable change. We in the social studies department doubted the capability of the English department and its members' commitment to our change initiatives. The breakup of the ITSS team marked the beginning of the dissolution of the change coalition in the high school. During the dissolution, the two departments did not openly talk about the strong feelings that all members of the ITSS team had about the termination. This lack of affective communication would become the standard way of dealing with our feelings about the actions of other people in the high school.

An Open Space Facility and an Open Classroom

Part of the original master plan was the construction of a new high school designed to accommodate the curricular and instructional innovations. In the spring of 1976, the senior high school finally moved to the new open-space facility. The core of the building included three completely open areas (social studies, library media center, and English) and three other areas that had occasional floor-to-ceiling demountable walls (business, math and science). The social studies department clustered its six teacher desks in the center of the open space, arranged all student desks into small group configurations that would accommodate two to six students per group, and put the storage cabinets around the periphery of the area.

In social studies, the open space proved to be a mixed blessing. It did provide greater flexibility for the teachers in managing the students as well as in matters of curriculum and instruction. The positioning of students at round tables or desk clusters kept the noise to a conversational level. However, any irregular behavior on the part of the students or teachers (for example, outbursts of laughter, the movement of groups of people) sent ripples of disruption throughout the open area. Teachers had to be continuously cognizant of the fact that their behavior would immediately affect the other 100 to 150 students and teachers in the room. Role playing, lectures, and audio-visual presentations had to take place in the lecture halls or the self-contained small-group rooms. Students sat close to the location of their materials to minimize movement. Students were not supposed to move; instead, teachers moved from table to table monitoring the group work and conducting conferences and oral testing.

The social studies faculty constantly critiqued the effectiveness of their procedures and regulations. They made philosophical and structural/procedural changes periodically, in their attempt to create a more efficient and effective learning environment. Due to the dedicated efforts of the social studies faculty, this open classroom with the mini-course curriculum lasted until 1989.

People as Agents of Change

The failure of educational change is a complicated affair, but the most often overlooked factors are the people who must implement the change (the teachers) and those who are often the objects of the change (the students and the teachers). These are the people who have the power to implement or resist. As previously mentioned, this school district's change attempt was a top-down initiative started by an assistant superintendent full of new ideas gained from a doctoral experience, a high school principal who also recently completed a doctorate, a new superintendent who agreed with the change agenda, and a group of teachers committed to substantive change.

Integral to this plan was the development of a master teacher program. Each of the major curricular areas had a master teacher who was to become the kindergarten through twelfth-grade instructional leader for that area. The role of the master teachers was to plan and carry out the major objectives of the master plan. Through a supplemental contract, they were paid an additional $1,000 annually; a substantial sum, especially in light of the 1969 starting teacher salary of $6,100. Master teachers were not administrators and had no administrative authority, therefore, the motivation of the principals and teachers in supporting the initiative was critical. Master teachers could discuss the merits of the changes and go into the classroom and demonstrate by teaching lessons, but they could not mandate or sanction.

In this group, the social studies master teacher shared the belief that change was necessary and that something better could be devised. Each of the other departments had a group of young and older teachers who were receptive to the idea of change. Through the efforts of a coalition including the administration, the master teachers, and many faculty members a community of discourse formed. However, students and parents, seen as the beneficiaries of the innovative research, knowledge, and effort of the educational professionals, were missing from this coalition. Rarely approached, even in an informal venue, students and parents were not part of the process that constructed the change. Instead, change was to be externally applied.

Sites of Imperviability and Resistance to Change

After one year, the English department withdrew from the ITSS program due to enrollment conditions and requirements. They went on to develop English mini-courses, which were taught in a more traditional manner, while the social studies department used the ITSS program as the basis for a ninth through twelfth-grade mini-course program that maintained the innovative curriculum, instruction, and assessment.

In the rest of the school district, resistance to some of the change initiatives started to grow. The social studies master teacher recalled that the initial source of resistance was the elementary teachers who had only a two-year college degree. As the more technical changes (for example, new instructional procedures for skill development and new curriculum packages) were brought into their classrooms, these elementary teachers resisted the changes because of the disruption of their established routines and the need to invest time in professional development. This attitude and behavior spread to other teachers and to some students, who were equally apprehensive about the ubiquitous change. Also, as the planning for the new high school was finalized, the math and science faculty developed reservations about teaching in an open environment, primarily because their instructional practices had not evolved to accommodate this new environment. In addition, the negative aspects of the English and social studies teaming experience in ITSS (for example, scheduling problems, staffing problems, and differences in philosophy and procedures) reinforced the conclusions of those who wanted to retain the traditional curriculum and mode of instruction.

Within the social studies department, concerns about teacher and student accountability led to behavioral adjustments that tightened the pedagogical routines. In their lesson planning and instructional practice, the teachers became more focused on student control. As the years unfolded, the department continued to address this concern by meticulously evaluating existing conditions and making adjustments including attempts to deal with fairness issues and instructional continuity among the teachers. The adjustments in the construction of learning packets, discipline procedures, grade reporting, classroom management procedures, and skill instruction (writing, speaking, and critical-thinking formats) invariably led to an increasing standardization of curriculum and instruction. Individual creativity was now possible only in curriculum planning and development activities on the department level, not on the instructional level where teacher/student interaction took place.

The adjustment decisions were always consensually decided. However, discussions prior to decision making became increasingly dialectical in that strong logical arguments, which could not be refuted by the others, would be put forward by some team members. For example, some of the social studies teachers strongly lobbied for an increasingly rigid standardization of curriculum and instruction, and they used the criticisms raised by students, parents, and administrators as the basis of their argument. The other members of the department found it difficult to empirically justify their positions, and therefore they conceded the points.

As the years passed, this difference of opinion led to the development of two factions—the three original members of the ITSS program and the rest of the department. The rest of the department was in agreement with the philosophy, but it was dissatisfied with the operational procedures. One outcome of this dissatisfaction was a lack of total commitment to the procedures and a growing laxity in their implementation on the part of the "rest of the department." The lack of commitment (or resistance to certain aspects of the program) was evident in such behavior as keeping sloppy records, ignoring student misbehavior, and not following agreed-upon curriculum, instructional procedures, and plans for the management of the open-space environment.

This was reminiscent of the social studies department's inability to deal openly with their emotional response to the disagreements with the English department concerning the termination of the ITSS program; the inability to emotionally confront others persisted within the social studies department between the original members and the rest of the department. The ensuing anger and resentment provided spaces for outside detractors of the program to attempt to influence the disaffected members of the department.

In 1976 the systematic nature of the school and an administrative change significantly affected the open-space change initiative. Shortly after moving into the open-space building, the faculty became aware of the systemic nature of an open-space facility. All of the departments except social studies maintained their traditional curriculum and instructional practices or began a return to traditional pedagogy. The open facility, in conjunction with teacher-directed instruction (that is, lectures, audio-visual presentations), resulted in noise, distraction, and off-task behavior. In many cases, to go to the restroom a student would have to walk through two or three other "classrooms." In any department area, audio-visual presentations, lectures, dramatic presentations, and so on would compete simultaneously for everyone's attention. As the years passed and the staff (including some of the social studies teachers) returned to traditional pedagogy, words like "cacophonous" and "bedlam" were used to describe the learning environment. Noise and distraction knew no boundary in this open-space facility. Sight and sound intermingled between classrooms and departmental areas.

Also in 1976, the assistant superintendent left the school district to assume a superintendency in another city. Many felt that this was the beginning of the end for the change initiatives. The new assistant superintendent was not part of the original coalition, and he showed his disregard for the open classroom by not even bothering to visit the social studies area. In a later conversation, he mentioned that there was no need to observe the environment because both of his children had experienced the social studies program and found it wanting as an effective educational environment. This attitude cemented the adversarial relationship between the social studies department and the administration; by this time the social studies department was the last nontraditional area in the school.

By 1979 an adversarial relationship had developed between the administration and the social studies department. The administration's concerns were centered on the nontraditional nature of the social studies program. Mastery learning, continuous progress, and student selection of courses based on interest were the main targets. Another administrative problem with the program concerned the nature of collaborative group work. Administrators questioned whether group evaluations and group grades were fair, and even whether students should be required to work with others.

The years from 1979 to 1983 witnessed two trends in the high school: a continuing attempt by the social studies faculty to withstand the growing criticism and the rapid movement of the rest of the school toward traditional practice. During this time, the social studies department attempted to meet the criticism by gradually changing its curriculum and instruction. In this process, the department eliminated student choice, gave more traditional names to its courses, and instituted more large-group teacher-centered courses. The rest of the school purged mini-courses, small-group work, and nontraditional assessment (oral and group) from their curriculum. The utilization of the open space clearly illustrated the remaining difference between social studies and the rest. The social studies area was still arranged in the wall-less, small-group configuration, while ineffectual makeshift walls that rose only to eye level separated the classrooms of the other areas.

Nineteen eighty-three was a bad year for the social studies program. The school underwent a Middle States evaluation that was sharply critical of the open classroom, and the evaluation committee called for an immediate return to the traditional use of space in order to accommodate a traditional curriculum. Further, the National Commission on Excellence in Education published *A Nation At Risk* (1983). This call for higher standards and "back to basics" fueled the fire of resistance to the social studies program. The social studies program was now viewed as the antithesis of excellence in education. Finally, the social studies master teacher retired. Not only was he the last of the master teachers, but he was the second last of the original planners of the change (only the superintendent remained). More important, social studies lost its most important defender. As a native of the area and a teacher for 35 years, his integrity and judgment were unquestionable. Many of the program's critics were held at bay by his reasoned and deliberate discourse. If losing the original assistant superintendent was the beginning of the end, the loss of this teacher was a definite sign of the imminent end of the program. Because of these events, the social studies department was now so estranged from the administration, staff, students, and parents that a bunker mentality took shape. The other departments viewed social studies as a threat to their pedagogy, and social studies was sharply critical of the other departments' capitulation to traditionalism.

The social studies department's provision, shortly thereafter, of an optional totally traditional track that any student could elect failed to stem the criticism. It was not enough that the social studies department continued to make concessions to the administration. During the 1989 school year, the administration ordered social studies to completely drop its unconventional program and return to a traditional program of teacher-centered curriculum and instruction. Gone were the small groups, quarter-credit mini-courses, simulations, and oral assessments. The norm became textbooks, students arranged in rows, lectures, worksheets, makeshift walls, and the passive watching of videos. Emotionally, the order to return to a traditional curriculum and instructional system was devastating. The years of hard work counted for naught, the department's self-esteem hit rock bottom, some of the department members felt that some of the other members betrayed them, and all members felt betrayed by the other departments in the school.

In 1994, the building was divided into traditional self-contained classrooms. Along with the renovation came outcome-based education (OBE). As mandated by the state of Pennsylvania, public schools were to incorporate portfolio assessment, write performance outcomes, and institute a high school graduation project in which all students must demonstrate their holistic mastery of the outcomes.

Ironically, the educational consultants, hired by the school district to train the faculty and implement the mandates, promoted much of the theory that was foundational to the social studies program of the open school. However, to the unspoken chagrin of the administration and to the resentful glee of the original members of the social studies department, the newly renovated building was not compatible with this new change.

Despite the apparent validation of their earlier pedagogy, the social studies department, along with the rest of the faculty, was skeptical about the mandates. The skepticism centered on the now pervasive question about how long this change would last.

To implement the mandates, the administration established an extensive committee system in which faculty were assigned to various committees and expected to participate actively. Much of the value of OBE, as perceived by the faculty and presented by the administration and consultants, was lost in the adversality fostered by the administrative demands on the teachers, by the teachers' resistance to the administration and to this change, and by the possibility that the changes would prove to be short-lived.

The adversality, along with a change in high school administration, fostered a political climate that eventually led to the termination of the committee system. This coincided with a political change in Pennsylvania. In 1998 the new governor formally ended OBE and initiated a statewide standards program. Gone, in our school, were the portfolios, outcomes, and holistic projects. Once again the politically driven pedagogical pendulum had swung.

A Study of Change and A New Direction

With the advent of outcome-based education (OBE) in Pennsylvania in the early 1990s, my efforts to implement an OBE-related curriculum in my classroom and high school led me to consulting work in other school districts. Viewing the process of change and the attitude of the administration and faculty in other districts toward the implementation of this change caused me to raise even more pessimistic questions and reach even more pessimistic conclusions about the efficacy of educational change. At this time, my reflections on my long personal experience with change resulted in the conclusions that change invariably fails, and that seemingly worthy ideas become ineffectual recycled fads. Moreover, I felt that educators were not only impotent in effecting change, but they could not even determine what would improve education.

These conclusions raised a number of questions. Why does change invariably fail? Why do individuals actively resist change? What are the conditions that would lead to successful change in education? What is successful change? Questions such as these coalesced into the three propositions about educational change that frame this research; modernistic professional development strategies are inadequate in dealing with change;

the lack of inclusion of teachers in policy making is a significant component in understanding the failure of change; and an examination of how teachers construct their meanings is necessary in constructing change.

My attempt to answer these questions led me to a master's degree program that provided opportunities to find answers through the objective quantification of my experience (Horn, 1995; 1999a). Yet this scientific approach failed to provide the definitive answers I sought. My pursuit of these answers next led to research at Pennsylvania State University research that culminated in this study.

My previously myopic view of educational change was improved by the study of critical pedagogy, postmodernism, systems theory and thinking, symbolic interactionism, semiotics, post-formalism, critical ethnography, critical examination of the history and development of education, and postmodern readings of spirituality. This expanded frame of reference provided new directions in which to construct the meaning of my experience and to participate with others in the examination of their experience.

These new directions resulted in the following question: Through the use of post-formal professional development strategies, can teachers develop the skills needed to deal with the issues of power that deny their inclusion in policy making? Can they develop a systemic view of their profession that, in turn, informs their practice? And can they gain the knowledge that facilitates a critical construction of their practice?

Chapter Two

A Post-Formal Inquiry

Critical reflection on my experience indicates that teachers are central to effective change. Their position in the hierarchy of education creates leverage opportunities in dealing with other stakeholders (specifically parents, students, and administrators). However, long-term change fails to occur for the following reasons: education is locked into a modernistic paradigm that is inappropriate for the postmodern problems education faces; teachers lack the power, skills, and knowledge to effect substantial change; and established professional development strategies perpetuate the two previously mentioned conditions.

These conclusions led to further questions. What understanding of change would career high school teachers who have shared the same change initiative construct? Through post-formal conversation, can teachers acquire the skills and knowledge that will inform their awareness and understanding of educational change? Can teachers become empowered through this post-formal process? Finally, is this post-formal process an appropriate professional development model for the postmodern condition?

Answering these questions necessitates an understanding of how career teachers view the change attempts in which they have participated. People other than teachers usually generate the countless theories and speculations concerning educational change. If teachers are central to an understanding of change, then an investigation is required into the interpretations and meanings that teachers construct about the change they experience.

My investigation has taken the form of a post-formal inquiry. One of the multiple purposes of *Teacher Talk* is to explicate and explore the potential of post-formal inquiry as an investigative and professional development model. An essential element of post-formal inquiry is the consideration of power. Power is seen as a ubiquitous entity that affects all meaning-making. This ubiquity of power leads to the premise that change cannot be fully understood unless all of the ramifications of power are uncovered, and relevant change cannot occur without the empowerment of the system's stakeholders. Relevant to educational systems is the post-formal belief that substantial educational change cannot occur without the empowerment of the teachers/gatekeepers and their subsequent use of this power.

Inquiry of a post-formal nature also recognizes the power of the researcher, the power to direct and mold participant interpretations, to frame the participants' stories in the researcher's agenda. My dual role of participant and researcher further complicates the issue of researcher power. Therefore, since I am using the narrative genre format of post-formal inquiry, which like any good story relies on the intuitive construction of the storyteller, I will attempt to disclose my biases and agenda as the story unfolds.

Antecedents

Post-formal inquiry is a qualitative method with the following antecedents: ethnography, interpretive/constructivist inquiry, critical ethnography, resistance postmodernistic qualitative research, and emancipatory or catalytic inquiry.

Ethnography has evolved from the initial task of describing a culture (Spradley, 1979) to the fourth-generation evaluation of Egon Guba and Yvonna Lincoln (1989) and the postmodern ethnography of Joe Kincheloe and Peter McLaren (1994). Egon Guba and Yvonna Lincoln's (1989) fourth-generation evaluation moves beyond mere description by proposing a blend of interpretivist philosophy with a call for social action. "Moving beyond the telling of stories, constructivism requires that evaluation catalyze social action" (Greene, 1994, p. 540). Kincheloe and McLaren (1994) add critical theory and postmodern uncertainty to the ethnographic method.

Ethnography is an antecedent of this study because of its many ways of informing our understanding of educational change. The theories that we construct about educational change are culture-bound in that when people learn a culture they are "living inside a particular reality that is taken for granted as 'the reality'" (Spradley, 1979, p. 10). Educational culture is a melange including high culture, popular culture, teacher culture, and local culture. All of these affect the construction of meaning and must be recognized as important components in the reconceptualization of educational change.

Ethnography provided an alternative to the positivistic testing of formal theories developed by empirical researchers. Historically, the theory of traditional ethnography allowed the development of theories "grounded in the empirical data of cultural description" (Spradley, 1979, p. 11). However, a critical, constructivist ethnography grounds the theory in the constructions of the participants (including the researcher) and in considerations of power. Constructivist ethnography sees reality as constructions shared among many individuals and cultures and is dependent on the interpretations of the involved individuals or groups (Guba & Lincoln, 1989). The interpretivist position relevant to my study is summarized by the statement that "we do not simply live out our lives *in* time and *through* language; rather we *are* our history" (Schwandt, 1994, p. 120). The implication that people are active constructors of reality is germane to an explanation of educational change that is centered on power. Another principle of constructivism, that the individual's constructions or reality are alterable, provides the potential for empowerment, especially since constructions are self-sustaining and self-renewing. The mere realization of the existence of this dynamic creates the potential for changing these constructions.

My study embeds constructivism in critical theory. Researchers who use critical theory to contextualize their research attempt to use their work as a form of social or cultural criticism, and base this criticism on the assumption "that all thought is fundamentally mediated by power relations that are socially and historically constituted" (Kincheloe & McLaren, 1994, p. 139). The significance of critical theory to my research is the assumption that resistance and a "political unconscious" (Kincheloe & McLaren, 1994, p. 140) lurk behind the narrative of educational change. Therefore, as people construct or deconstruct their narratives about educational change, this construction/interpretation process must acknowledge the context of power.

In addition, ethnography accommodates the systemic complexity of societies as well as the individual human behavior within those societies by allowing an examination of specific elements of a situation within a holistic context. Methodologically, ethnography requires the sustained presence of the researcher to the culture under study. The participants in my research project and I interacted professionally for 30 years. The descriptive aspect of ethnography is evident in this study in that all of the participants engaged in the construction of the story. However, my research was not solely ethnographic since its purposes required a broader type of inquiry than that provided for by descriptive ethnography.

My research not only avoided the purely descriptive process of ethnography but also the disingenuous form of critical ethnography that objectifies and reifies the participants. This deleterious form of critical ethnography occurs when the researcher first describes the participants' interpretations of their experience and then compares their interpretations to critical theory, resulting in a judgmental resolution of their experience in light of the theory (Kincheloe & McLaren, 1994). My work assiduously attempted to maintain an interpretivist and constructivist ethnographic philosophy of research. The essential activity in this research was not to describe participant opinions and attitudes but to elicit participant assumptions and to challenge them through the interjection of relevant theory, through the commentary of the other participants, and through critical questions posed by the researcher.

The critical component of *Teacher Talk* is the inclusion of the historical, social, and economic aspects of educational change (Fontana & Frey, 1994). The inclusion of the ubiquity of power is essential to the critical construction of educational change. *Teacher Talk* realizes "that all thought is fundamentally mediated by power relations that are socially and historically constituted" (Kincheloe & McLaren, 1994, p. 139). This realization, along with the epiphanies that resulted from interpretive interactions (Fontana & Frey, 1994) through the post-formal conversation, created transformative possibilities for the participants and for me.

This post-formal inquiry was dynamically influenced by the resistance postmodernistic qualitative theory as described by Kincheloe and McLaren: "postmodern ethnographic writing faces the challenge of moving beyond simply the re-animation of local experience, an uncritical celebration of cultural difference, and the employment of a framework that espouses universal values and a global role for interpretivist anthropology" (1994, p. 153). One goal of my research was to "challenge dominant Western research practices that are underwritten by a foundational epistemology and a claim to universally valid knowledge at the expense of local, subjugated knowledges" (Kincheloe & McLaren, 1994, p. 153). This goal proved to be difficult to achieve, as described in the participants' stories in Chapter Five.

A final antecedent of post-formal inquiry is the catalytic or emancipatory inquiry espoused by Patti Lather. Catalytic inquiry is relevant for my purposes because it "moves those it studies to understand the world and the way it is shaped in order for them to transform it" (Kincheloe & McLaren, 1994, p. 152). The intent of post-formal conversation is to empower the participants and motivate them to take critical action. Lather reconceptualizes validity for "praxis-oriented researchers" who wish to conduct "research that is openly committed to a more just social order" (1986, p. 270). Methodologically, Lather proposes an unorthodox type of validity—catalytic validity. In keeping with the relational and emancipatory aspects of critical research, "catalytic validity represents the degree to which the research process reorients, focuses, and energizes participants toward knowing reality in order to transform it" (Lather, 1986, p. 272). This direction or purpose of research is fundamentally different from the positivistic, value-neutral modernistic research paradigm in that the purpose of research is "the desire to consciously channel this impact so that respondents gain self-understanding and, ultimately, self-determination through research participation" (Lather, 1986, p. 272). The effectiveness of this study in relation to catalytic validity will be discussed in Chapter Five.

Trustworthiness

This post-formal inquiry was not centered on quantitative constructions and methods but rather on people interacting with each other and on the ways these interactions affected their constructions of meaning. Quantitative research techniques were inappropriate because their inordinate attention to technique prevents the more important issue of purpose from taking center stage (Kincheloe, 1999). The qualitative purpose was catalytic, not descriptive, because of the interpretive and constructionist nature of my post-formal purpose; the quantitative concern of validity was replaced by a concern for trustworthiness.

Kincheloe proposes that trustworthiness is a better assessment measure of critical constructivist research than validity is. Trustworthiness is established through an assessment of the "credibility of portrayals of constructed realities" (Kincheloe, 1991, p. 135) and the replacement of external validity with anticipatory accommodation. Anticipatory accommodation is a Piagetian-like condition in which the researcher and participants move beyond the levels of problem solving and critically reflective thinking to a reshaping of their "cognitive structures to accommodate unique aspects of what is being perceived in new contexts" (Kincheloe, 1991, p. 136).

In a post-formal inquiry, the reshaping of cognitive structures would be evident when the participants and the researcher incorporated new concepts and strategies in the construction of their experience. In an educational context, anticipatory accommodation would be evident when teachers who previously did not include concepts such as power, systems thinking, teacher culture, conversational types, and affect control theory now included these concepts in their construction of meaning. Additionally, anticipatory accommodation could include evidence of a reshaping of the cognitive processes used in constructing meaning in that critical reflection on experience, psychoanalytic analysis of place (Kincheloe and Pinar, eds. 1991), currere (a method of critical autobiographical reflection) (Pinar, 1994), or critical action research would become part of the teacher's repertoire. Despite the Piagetian emphasis on cognition, the affective considerations inherent in these reflective practices must be viewed as equally important parts of the process of anticipatory accommodation.

Gary Anderson addresses validity similarly, in the critical comment that "educational researchers have been moving to systematize ethnographic research in an attempt to make it more scientific, often even invoking the language of positivism to do so" (1989, p. 252). In this case, "methodological rigor" is promoted more than "the creative act of researcher interpretation" (Anderson, 1989, p. 252). Anderson recognizes the "openly ideological research" that critical ethnographers carry out and the fact that "trustworthiness" can be enhanced through member checking and the triangulation of data sources and methods. In addition, credibility can be heightened by basic procedures like audit trails, interview guides, making reports available to informants, following the verbatim principle, using an expanded account of field notes, and keeping a fieldwork journal (Janesick, 1994; Patton, 1990; Spradley, 1979). Chapter Four will contain a detailed analysis of how these procedures were used to enhance the trustworthiness of this research.

In *Teacher Talk*, trustworthiness and verification are construed in this manner. If the stories about the participants' constructions were considered accurate by the participants, then they were deemed trustworthy. The verification process secured this trustworthiness by including all participants in the interpretive processes. However, the trustworthiness and verification were expanded to include the emancipatory paradigm of Lather in that "our goal in research is not merely to validate the statistical relationship of variables but is to understand, to make intelligible, and to preserve the cohesiveness of the phenomena being studied" (1992, p. 89). Lather's emancipatory paradigm of inquiry leads both the researcher and the informant along Kincheloe's path to empowerment.

Trustworthiness, as it arises out of the data-gathering and analysis procedures, is a political statement about research. Lather's description of an experience in data gathering shows the difference between modern and post-formal research intentions: "sequential interviews conducted in an interactive, dialogic manner that entails self-disclosure on the part of the researcher foster a sense of collaboration; and group interviews provide tremendous potential for deeper probing and reciprocally educative encounter" (1988, p. 574). Researcher self-disclosure, collaboration, and interactive deep probing are central to the emancipatory intent of post-formal inquiry. As described later in this chapter, both sequential dialogic interviews and group interviews were used to foster trustworthiness.

Post-Formal Inquiry: A Definition

Like ethnography, post-formal inquiry includes a sustained researcher presence and a description of experience and situation. As in interpretivist and constructivist ethnography, the purpose of the post-formal researcher's presence is to participate in and to facilitate the participant's description and construction of the experience and situation. As in critical ethnography, power in its historical, social, and economic contexts is central to an understanding of educational change. As in resistance postmodernistic qualitative research, dominant Western research practices and their claims and consequences are challenged. And, as in catalytic or emancipatory inquiry, the success of post-formal inquiry is determined by "the degree to which the research process reorients, focuses, and energizes participants toward knowing reality in order to transform it" (Lather, 1986, p. 272).

Trustworthiness established through collegial collaboration is the essence of validity and verifiability in post-formal inquiry. Researcher and participants work together to construct, critically reflect upon, and reconstruct an understanding of the past, present, and future. Trustworthiness implies that all are equal participants with the researcher holding no interpretive power over the participants.

Additionally, post-formal inquiry requires the inclusion of an understanding of the postmodern context of current human activity, the use of dialogic conversation, an awareness of the dynamic and holistic characteristics of systems, an engagement of theory and practice in the context of Paulo Freire's praxis (Freire & Macedo, 1996), an awareness of the effects of the institutionalization of education, and a conscious engagement with affect control theory. All of this knowledge and skill must drive the underlying purpose of the inquiry, which is to facilitate the growth of the participants as critically conscious and empowered individuals.

Synergy

Unlike positivistic research and some forms of qualitative inquiry, post-formal inquiry requires a synergistic relationship between the researcher and the participants. Working together in an egalitarian manner, their combined effect is greater than their individual effects. A post-formally created synergy does not imply that the result will be consensus. The goal is to facilitate the development of more complex collective interpretations in relation to the topic under inquiry. Post-formal inquiry proposes that, to attain this synergetic state, participant roles, collegial collaboration, and catalysts must be carefully crafted and included in the inquiry.

Participant Roles

The researcher is a participant. This role can best be described by looking at the role of the participants. The names used to identify those who take part in research/inquiry clarify the distinction between the ways in which these people are viewed in different types of research. Post-formal inquiry uses the term "participant" because this person is an equal partner in the process, whereas the quantitative term "subject" implies a fallacious relationship in which the researcher is a value-neutral, objective observer of the person's behavior. The researcher/subject relationship is characterized in terms of superior and subordinate. The qualitative term "informant" also implies a distinction between the researcher and the participant, in that they are separated by function and by access to information or the construction of information. In post-formal inquiry there is no separation by function or information construction. Both researcher and participants engage in a free "give and take" of information (function) and collaboratively participate in the construction of meaning.

Post-Formal Inquiry and Collegial Collaboration

Unlike traditional professional development models, post-formal inquiry strives for collegial collaboration between the person conducting the professional development and the participants. Interview formats and sequences, data collection procedures and their use in analysis, and how information was shared were aspects of the inquiry that were designed to promote collegial collaboration.

To promote post-formal inquiry, the following techniques were used: the use of feedback papers as a way to introduce theory and to extend the conversation, the challenging of prior assumptions, and reflection on current issues in the participant's school.

Interview Format and Sequence
Teacher Talk created a condition of collegial collaboration through the following activities and procedures. A series of interviews was conducted, providing an opportunity for the teachers to reflect upon their educational experience in the past, present, and future and in relation to the place in which they teach. The interviews made use of open-ended questions to "make it possible for the person being interviewed to bring the interviewer into his or her world" (Patton, 1990, p. 279). The most open-ended approach to interviewing, an informal conversational interview or unstructured interview, was used to maintain maximum flexibility and minimum researcher directedness (Patton, 1990; Fontana & Frey, 1994). The benefit was two-fold: it allowed participants to independently pursue what was relevant to each of them, and it allowed insight into the individual construction of shared experience. Also, where a fragmented or disparate collective reality concerning the same experience emerged, open-ended interviewing allowed an analysis of the different constructions.

The initial questions I posed were of an open-ended nature, allowing the participant to establish a relevant direction. The questions were as follows: Has change in education affected your life? What do you think would be some important questions about educational change? What would you like to know about educational change? How have you been involved in educational change? What do you do that represents change? Follow-up questions for each interview were determined by the participant's answers. In other words, each interview developed within the framework of the questions and answers generated by the participants (interviewer and interviewee), not in relation to any predetermined standardized format.

After the first interview, the following questions were added to the original list: Ideally, how should change be handled? How much contact do you have (have you had) with educational theory? How often do you interact with other teachers? Is this type of conversation (what we are doing) valuable in promoting change? How do you "feel" about this interview and the interview process as we are doing it? What is the difference between new teachers today and when we were new teachers? What direction will your pedagogy take in the future?

After each interview I produced a transcript and gave it to the participant. The next interview started with a review of the transcript of the previous meeting. At this time the participant could correct any inaccuracies, reconstruct or embellish any prior constructions. The number of separate interviews varied with each participant, as did the length of time of the interviews. Each participant was initially interviewed for approximately two hours. Two of the participants had two formal interviews, and the other three had one.

Other interactions between the participants and me included my feedback documents; the participants' written and informal conversational responses to my feedback; a sharing of all written documents (transcripts, feedback papers), including my journals; informal conversations between the participants; a group conversation involving four participants and myself; a meeting of three of the participants and myself to create an in-service proposal for the administration; and participant checking of the written research. The documents in the appendixes are given in slightly edited form.

Data Collection Procedures and Their Use in Analysis

All interviews were tape-recorded, and transcripts were generated for purposes of analysis. Transcripts were given to the participants for their review. The use of transcripts between interviews allowed the participants and myself to critically reflect on what was said, and this enhanced the quality of the next interview. Initially, participants only received transcripts of their own interview; however, after the first round of interviews the participants decided to pass around the transcripts.

The procedure of providing transcripts enhanced the trustworthiness of the information, provided for less reactive constructions, and expedited more developed responses. In terms of the earlier discussion of anticipated accommodation, providing the transcripts facilitated the reshaping of our cognitive structures.

My analysis of the transcribed conversation and the notes that I had taken during the conversation were structured in the form of four journals. These journals had the dual purpose of facilitating my analysis and interpretation of what was happening, and of providing the theory and questions that would broaden the participants' consciousness and challenge their assumptions. Even though the journals were shared with the participants, pertinent journal information reappeared in the feedback papers and member-checking activities in order to broaden their awareness of a situation or challenge a specific assumption. For example, Appendix A was a debriefing document that I introduced into the conversation at the end of the research period. Appendix A was created from my journal information and represents a member-checking technique that allowed me to assess the veracity of my own interpretations, as well as once again allowing me to challenge the participants to broaden their awareness of certain issues. This dual purpose can also be seen in Appendix B, which was the feedback paper given to Barry after his first interview. This feedback paper was generated entirely from my journals (which represented my analysis of the first interview). Appendixes C and D were also generated in this manner for these dual purposes.

I maintained one journal containing information related to the interviews. A section of this journal was dedicated to the documentation of my role and decisions, and it provided informative commentary on the reasons for my decisions concerning such issues as question selection, the selection of information and the timing of its introduction, and the selection of one segment of transcribed conversation over another. I did this to keep track of my actions and intents. Another function of this journal was to track my consistent pursuit of answers to questions. What does a person *do* that represents change? Were the participants taking on the language of critical examination but maintaining old practices? Did the participants feel that this process facilitated or supported further change? This journal was shared with the participants and used during the interviews to clarify constructions made by the participants or myself.

I kept a second journal that was solely dedicated to professional development and affective considerations. Throughout the individual interview sequence, I analyzed data to discern categories, relationships, and patterns that would inform my understanding of this inquiry as professional development and the affective aspects of this process. As emotions and remembrances of emotions occurred in the research, I invited participants to explicate these situations and reflect on the place of emotion in the change process. This journal was also shared with the participants, and it was used during the interviews to clarify constructions made by the participants or myself.

A third journal dealt with my own constructions about what was discussed. The purpose of this journal was to track the evolution of my thinking concerning the theory that is explicated throughout this story, and how this theory changed because of my interaction with the constructions of the other participants. The story that was told by this journal recognized the partiality of my own narrative within the narratives that we collectively constructed. Such narratives are inevitably partial "in the sense that they are unfinished, imperfect, limited; and partial in the sense that they project the interests of 'one side' over others. Because those voices are partial and partisan, they must be made problematic" (Ellsworth, 1989, p. 305). The acceptance of the partiality of our constructions required a concomitant struggle with this phenomenon, which was facilitated by the journal. This information was shared with the participants as deemed relevant in the context of the feedback papers.

In addition, I maintained a conversation chronology detailing what happened and when it happened. Another record that I kept dealt with the ideas generated by the participants about the procedures and directions of this research. This record included such information as Dave's initiation of the idea of passing around transcripts, Barry's suggestion of a culminating group conversation, Dan's suggestion of a group roundtable discussion, and Sue's proposal that the group should meet to expand the conversation to the rest of the faculty and that an in-service proposal involving this kind of conversation should be presented to the administration. Also, some of the participants used analogies to explain their experience. Therefore, I kept a record of these analogies and the context in which they appeared.

Finally, a journal called the "Glossary of Theory" was kept to keep track of when theory was interjected into the conversation. This journal detailed the theory included in the feedback papers and recorded its introduction to the various participants.

Information Sharing

To promote egalitarian collegiality and to guard against the specter of expertism, I made available to the participants any and all of my information that could inform our inquiry. This included my research proposal, documentation related to the information in the proposal, and primary source documents about the change experiences shared by the participants as detailed in Chapter One. These sources ranged from curriculum guides to informal communications. Open availability and disclosure of all information was central in establishing the trust that is inherent in an egalitarian relationship between researcher and participant.

Ironically, the participants made virtually no requests for this information. At one point, Sue expressed a desire to learn more about the effects of postmodernism on education; I responded by providing her with Andy Hargreaves' book (1994). Besides this, the participants did not request any other information. My initial speculation was that this lack of interest was a reflection of their distrust of theory. I sensed that they valued the interaction of their own interpretations more than any theory that I could provide. The affective component of their remembrances undoubtedly reinforced the veracity of these memories and the new meanings constructed by this analysis of their past and present experience. Often the inability of theory to invoke emotion is to the detriment of the believability of the theory.

In the first member-checking activity to verify my own speculations, I asked about their lack of requests for theoretical information (Appendix A). Sue responded in writing:

> I didn't pursue a lot of theoretical information because of two reasons:
>
> A. I diligently read the transcripts and the commentaries that you provided. The commentaries were steeped in theoretical information that was well-chosen and easy to digest. You selected relevant information and made it very understandable. For my own purposes, it sufficed.
>
> B. Time—as much as I'd like to do (and should do) more "professional" reading, I just don't make it a priority. So much *necessary* professional reading crosses my desk that I don't usually opt to do additional reading.

In an interview Barry responded with this comment:

> Well your assessment is probably correct. It is one thing to talk about things in theory, but it is another to deal with it in reality. I think that most teachers with any experience have dealt with so much theory that they really don't give it the credibility that it may deserve. I think most teachers today want to deal with reality—the way that things really are, not the way things should or could be.

Dave's response was as follows:

> I guess at this point in my career with a limited time to go [until retirement] there is nothing that I could read that would change my approach to education, or how I feel about education. It would be nice fluff reading if I had the time, which I don't. So it is just real low in priority.

Steve had this to say about not requesting theoretical information:

> It's interesting to think and talk about theory and even to read it, but it becomes an issue of prioritizing your time. I feel guilty about this because I just don't have time to sit and reflect about theory. Theory needs that kind of reflection, and I can't do it during my job. To request theory means extra work. It would be an assignment that you have to do that competes with the stuff that needs to be done for school. You can't grade tomorrow's papers or get the test typed on the computer if you read theory. So theory is a luxury that I can't afford. You know, thinking about talking about theory conjures up the notion of [engaging in] a luxurious past time. Theory tends to be put off, and I feel bad about it because this is what we should be doing.

Dan's response to this issue was similar to the others' responses:

You are right on the distrust of theory; you are right on target for me on that one. The one thing that I would say is that more than a lack of interest, it is more a lack of time. I just don't get around to a lot of things that I should do.

Ray: Would you be more interested in theory if there was time provided during the school day for faculty to get together and pursue theory, or does that still turn you off?

Dan: If it were in a small discussion group type of format I think that I would enjoy that. Sitting in a whole faculty meeting and talking about theory, I know I would zone out. In particular if it is a late afternoon. Also, it would have to be interactive.

Dan's response to the value of the feedback papers followed the same theme:

Dan: I will be honest with you again—I scanned them. This was because of the time factor. I prioritize everything, and this is low priority.

The documentation that I could provide was not forced on the participants because, in addition to believing in the decision-making capabilities of the participants, post-formal inquiry recognizes the value of the participants' indigenous knowledge and the participants' ability to create more complex cognitive structures from a critical examination of that knowledge. However, as pointed out by the participants, time to reflect on theory in relation to one's practice is a scarce commodity. The participants tended to see theory as an entity separate from their practice. The inclusion of selected theory in the context of their reflections on their practice (in the feedback papers, as well as in the conversation) proved effective in dealing with the issues of time to deal with theory, theory informing practice, and theory promoting praxis (Freire & Macedo, 1996). As shown in Appendix B, the theory presented was in the form of short relevant profiles. I provided no long excerpts from documents or bibliography of historical and theoretical texts to the participants. My intuition was that they would not read anything that was time consuming.

Feedback Papers

After every interview or group conversation, I provided the participant(s) with a document called a "feedback paper," containing three types of information: my opinions on and reactions to what they said, theory and other information relevant to what they said, and questions about what they said, or about what they said in the context of the information that I introduced. The feedback papers that I generated after every conversation not only provided a way to extend the conversation but also provided a way for me to introduce relevant theory into the conversation. The standard opening of every feedback paper described this process:

> The following comments are my reflections on this interview. To facilitate an understanding of what I mean, if I use a technical word, I will provide a definition or explanation of the word or idea. If you wish to read more about the idea, I can provide more information. Also, for convenience I will bold the technical/theory words.

For instance, in my feedback paper after Barry's first interview I introduced theoretical information on a number of topics (see Appendix B). The information on teacher culture was later communicated to the other participants in feedback papers, but only when relevant to their own construction of meaning. When the group decided to exchange transcripts, we also exchanged feedback papers. This exchange of feedback papers not only reinforced the information for participants who had previously been exposed to it, but also introduced others to the information in an authentic context.

The mechanism within the feedback papers that was used to extend the conversation was my proposing follow-up questions in response to what the person said or in response to my own interpretations of what the person said. For instance, in the paper giving feedback to Barry's first interview, my response included follow-up questions (see Appendix B). When were these questions answered? Some of the questions became follow-up questions asked in the next interview, others were discussed in informal hallway or lunch time conversations, and others were merely answered in the mind of the participant.

The effectiveness of this questioning technique in expanding the conversation was hard to determine in relation to the more formalized questioning and answering in the succeeding conversations. When asked about the effectiveness of using this technique, Sue offered: "I did think about them, and they frequently caused a lot of introspection. The feedback papers were valuable self-evaluative tools." Steve felt the same way and reiterated his concern about time:

> I think the questions were good. The questions and everything were valuable, but again it requires a certain amount of time to reflect on them. You must actually think about them as opposed to something that we just hear about, which requires reflection. There is very little time in the professional day to deal with any kind of reflective thought and any kind of theory. Did I think about them? Yes for about five or ten minutes prior to the conversation. Once the conversation was over I tended to put it on the back burner.

I asked Dave if he would be more likely to consider theory if it were brought out in conjunction with these follow-up questions:

> Yes, if the person while talking about a question in an on-going dialogue were presenting theory, it would be fun to talk about. But for me to actually take the time to sit down in isolation and read a book about theory, not very likely. You know there was a big gap between when we talked and when I got the feedback questions, so I lost my train of thought. Also, I didn't have anybody to talk to about them; which is what I would rather do. So the questions were merely something for me to ponder, and that was about it. They would have been much more effective if you would have been there to talk with me.

Barry also felt that the feedback papers and questions were effective:

> I think they were effective because I found them interesting to see other people's viewpoints. They brought up new ideas or different points of view in my mind. The questions, yes, I did think about them. I benefited in seeing what other people had to say. The questions and the papers made me aware of some things of which I wasn't aware. They expanded my knowledge base.

Challenging Prior Assumptions

Two recurring themes in all of the interviews that will be discussed in detail in Chapter Five involved the difference between young and old teachers and the difference between the "good old days" and the current situation. I wanted to challenge the assumptions that the participants held about the different behavior and attitudes of teachers with fewer or more years of experience and their assumptions about the difference in climate between the 1970s and the 1990s in their school. Therefore, I raised the issue of the dynamics of teacher career stages. In a feedback document addressed to Sue (that all participants received) I identified these recurring themes and included a reprint of information on teacher career stages (Fessler, 1995). This information included a model that dealt with serenity, conservatism, and bitterness, together with a career cycle model that included career wind-down and career exit stages. My implication was that perhaps our current constructions of meaning were merely indicative of a certain aspect of a certain career stage.

I raised this issue in the first group conversation, after the group had reached a consensus on the problems of education being caused by the lack of standards and by student inability to take responsibility for their learning. I asked if their conclusions reflected how things really were, or if their remarks just reflected the fact that they were at the end of their careers. This question prompted a conversation in which they attempted to justify their opinions by providing additional information and in which they critically reflected on the accuracy of their interpretations. Dan, who is the English department chairperson and mentor for new English teachers, responded in this manner:

> I think our conclusion is reality. In talking with some of the younger teachers I'm hearing some of these same frustrations from people who've only been teaching two or three years. Now they don't have the experience of comparing today's students to students in the past, but a remark that I've repeatedly heard is, when I was in high school I didn't realize that there was that body of students out there doing nothing, like they are today.

Barry wondered whether his conclusions were how things really were or had been reached "because I'm seeing it [school] through 30-year-old experienced eyes?"

On the other hand Steve assessed his situation in this manner:

> I've always thought that I am a reasonably good social observer, and I don't consider myself as being at the end of my career. Because I have always been kind of a workaholic, and because I have always had that kind of drive; I'm not looking for opportunities to screw off because I'm merely hanging out. I'm working harder and doing more in my classes than many of my students. I still do a lot of preparation; I do a lot more thinking. When I compare myself to a typical class, I am more willing to work than they are. When the students come in the room, their heads are down on the desk as soon as they walk in the door. We work through the moaning and groaning about how we work too hard. They complain: "I had to work last night, I had to work over the weekend." But anyway, my point is that I don't regard my observations as the observations of somebody who is ready to check out. If I was at the end of my career I would say forget it—who cares? But I think that this is not the case with me.

Steve's response is interesting in that the question caused him to evaluatively reflect on his dedication to the job as defined (by him) as the teacher's amount of preparation. Steve validated his position on the old teacher/new teacher issue through a reflective analysis of his current effort.

The inclusion of the career information prompted a deeper reflection on the participants' prior assumptions. Perhaps their resistance to the career stage information was generated by the suggestion that we are in the last stage of our careers. The insertion of theory throughout this post-formal inquiry caused the participants to either assimilate or accommodate the new information.

Inserting Current School Events into the Conversation

As situations that were related to our conversational issues occurred in our school, they were introduced into the conversation either through inclusion in the feedback papers or through my questioning during conversations. These situations included administrative actions during faculty meetings; comments in minutes submitted to the faculty by faculty committees; incidents involving other teachers and students; and the actions taken by the teachers' union. I contextualized these current issues in terms of past practice, issues of power, a systemic perspective, and emotional aspects. I also placed the discussion of these issues within the additional context of relevant theory that had already been introduced. Besides the sense of immediacy created by the inclusion of these issues, authenticity was enhanced by the added emotional impact.

The Synergetic Power of Post-Formal Inquiry

The synergetic power of post-formal inquiry was illustrated when out of one of these situations came Sue's idea to have our conversational group make an in-service proposal to the administration. The decision by the participants to expand their conversational format beyond the original group offered a significant validation of post-formal inquiry. Also, this action was significant because the decision constituted a synergetic effect arising out of the following post-formal techniques:

- The foundation for participant interest and trustworthiness was laid in the initial individual interviews.
- The group conversation facilitated the formation of a collective critique and interpretation of in-service programs.
- The use of a recent current event at a faculty meeting authentically focused the deeper issues of teacher empowerment and teacher action.
- The transcript allowed each participant to ruminate on each other participant's position.
- The feedback paper posed questions that focused the participants' attention on this issue.
  The sense of ownership felt by the participants allowed them to propose and organize this action.

Three members of the conversation group drafted a written proposal that was formally presented to the administration through a faculty advisory group (Faculty Planning) that regularly meets with the administration. None of the participants are members of the advisory group. The administration and faculty responded very favorably, and they reached a decision to schedule several sessions for the next school year.

The interaction of these techniques created a synergistic effect that proved to be greater in empowering and motivating the participants than the individual techniques used in isolation. The evolution of this synergy can be seen in the transcribed conversation.

Prior to the drafting of the proposal, toward the end of the first group conversation I made a statement that no matter what the issue, whether an issue such as high school discipline that involves the total faculty or a social studies issue involving only the social studies department "we (as total faculty, or as an individual department) have been able to come together and formulate plans consensually and develop actions everyone wants to take. Now why can't we do this for other issues—like pedagogical concerns, or things like scheduling that affect our pedagogy?" Barry agreed that we should be able to come together to deal with other issues. At that point, I introduced an incident that had occurred at a recent faculty meeting:

Ray: Now I want to ask Sue. At the last faculty meeting, Sue asked a question about next year's in-service days and who has input into the determination of the content of those days. And of course the answer from the principal was that the administration makes these decisions. And while all that interplay was going on, I looked across the room and I saw all of you sitting there. All of you who have been talking about dialogic conversation and sharing transcripts, and I wondered who could make a better decision about in-service, the central administration, a kindergarten through twelfth-grade committee established by the administration, or the people in that room at that faculty meeting.

Barry: It is logical for me that the people in that room are the ones who should be deciding what in-service is needed, not someone who sits down in the central office and has no contact whatsoever. It seems quite obvious who should make those decisions.

Ray: What was your intent behind that question, Sue?

Sue: Exactly what you said. I want to back up to this whole idea of in-servicing. Part of me wants to believe that when administrators are sitting down and facing a new school year, they have a lot of things to do, and one is to fill up the in-service time. I don't really get a sense that this is something that they are really psyched about. I get the feeling that it is like, "well we have five days to fill, and one of them is the opening of school, another is the closing of school; so what are we going to do to fill these other days?" I don't get the sense that there is some ultimate plot to fill up our time with nonsensical stuff, or stuff in which we have no interest. I think that there is a possibility that they might be relieved if a group would approach them and say, "Listen up, we have been looking at the in-service days, and we really think that maybe it would be a good idea to do this and that." I'm wondering when did anybody ever go to them. We are like Steve said—we are like sheep. We'll go to these in-service days and think that they are dumb, but next year we just do the same thing. When has a group ever gotten together and said, hey, let's sit down and think about something that we can do, and then gone to them and say—how about on these three days we would really like to try this. They might be relieved.

Barry: My suggestion to you would be rather than relieved, they would be threatened, because they often react as they did this past summer when we went to them and offered to have a committee on discipline to work with them. Their response was—"we'll do that, that's our job." And again I think their reaction was that way because they feel threatened. The power thing. I think they would feel threatened rather than relieved because it would be another instance of where teachers are trying to take some of their power.

Dan: I think that in addition to being threatened by power, they are also concerned by the public perception of what is an in-service day. I think that they [the administration] think that everybody has to be accountable, and again we are back to being herded like sheep through the whole thing whether we need it or not. What benefit do a lot of those meetings have where everyone has to go? What is wrong is that all employees have to be treated the same way, whether you are the school nurse or whether you are the classroom teacher.

Barry: I think Sue's 100 percent correct. I think that in-service should be generated by a faculty committee or a faculty/administration committee, as long as faculty and administration have an equal say. I think we should have input, but we never do.

Sue: But you know, if you set up a committee what you wind up having is a committee doing exactly what they are doing—having artificial kinds of things to fill up the time. The committee's going to look around to the intermediate unit or they are going to look around at those in-service people [experts]. The other thing is I didn't really even realize myself how much of a need we have for dialogue until I started going through these sessions with Ray. It has become so crystal clear to me that we are really lacking that [dialogue], and that it would be such a vehicle for professional development. What a vehicle for professional development this would be if we were able to dialogue with other people who are professionals.

After this conversation, I immediately responded to the participants with a feedback paper that included a summation and a list of questions about the in-service issue (see Appendix C). Sue immediately replied to this feedback, and I duplicated her response and circulated it to the rest of the participants. The questions and Sue's responses to them follow below:

a. Would our purpose include developing a conversation with other teachers (especially less experienced ones), pursuing the in-service recommendations idea and involving ourselves in other issues that traditionally have been in the purview of the administration?
I definitely think we should approach the administration about in-service ideas, thereby extending to all other staff the opportunity for meaningful, professional discussion. Hopefully, this would develop into meaningful professional development.
b. Who would be included in our conversations?
If it were presented as an in-service program, it should be one of a few options. I believe that interest in the group would grow then by "word of mouth." It could start small and take off from there. Initially, we should "stick together," but if there is growing interest, we could break into smaller groups.
c. Would our group become more formalized in its form and function?
We could see as we go.
d. What is our vision?
Continuous, meaningful professional development and support.
e. How can we sustain our group (find time to keep it going)?
Good question. I certainly will make myself available whenever possible because what we are doing is important. (How about a weekend retreat—Ha!)
f. How can we make this a fun thing as well as being professionally relevant?
We could meet socially as well as professionally.
g. Concerning Steve's idea that education is about asking questions, what other questions should we raise?
We would definitely poll interested faculty about issues that concern them, and use those as a starting point for further discussion.

After this response was circulated, Sue suggested that we set up a meeting to plan a proposal to be presented to the administration. This action was a direct result of the synergetic effects of the post-formal techniques more specifically the empowering outcome of post-formal conversation. The purpose of these catalytic techniques was realized in that it provided an opportunity for the participants to expand the context of how they view change. These techniques promoted the development of new connections in the participants, a critical constructivist process of understanding change. This broader perspective increased the potential for future intuitive insight and synthetical moments (Pinar, 1994) similar to the one that Sue had when "it became crystal clear."

Conclusion

This research method was crafted specifically to address the premise that long-term change fails to occur for the following reasons: education is locked into the modernistic paradigm, which is inappropriate for the postmodern problems that education faces; teachers lack the power, skills, and knowledge to effect substantial change; and established professional development strategies perpetuate the two previously mentioned conditions.

The role of post-formal inquiry is to mediate between the modern and the postmodern. Solutions to educational problems require the appropriate application of modernistic and postmodern techniques and ideology. Oxymoronically, the modern and the postmodern are not theoretically compatible; however, within our educational system they are irrevocably intertwined. Post-formal inquiry is proposed as a mechanism and a "way of being" that can critically accommodate these two dueling paradigmatic conditions.

Central to this method is the imperative of the equitable inclusion of teachers in policy making, and the belief that teachers need to engage in post-formal conversation in order to construct and critique their meanings about their professional lives and about educational change. Due to their position in the hierarchy of education, teachers can be the critical purveyors of the post-formal techniques that permit an accommodation to the postmodern condition that is so evident in American schools.

Chapter Three

Education in Crisis: The Postmodern Context

Criticism of American Education

The debate about the effectiveness of education has gone beyond the question of whether there is a problem. Critics paint bleak pictures of the effectiveness of American education. The perception is that reform is generally ineffective or at best episodic and local in its successes. The acrimonious debates within the educational community are not perceived by the public as esoteric debates within the realm of academia but as proof that educators do not know what they are doing. This perception is a high-profile politicized concern of the general public, shaped by special interest groups and ambitious politicians.

From a political and public contemporary viewpoint, educational reform does not have a good track record (Smith, 1995; Branson, 1987). After the Education Summit at Palisades, New York, *Newsweek* columnist Jonathan Alter rejoiced in the fact that with a few exceptions, educators were left out of the conference. Alter continued his commentary on education as a "sea of mediocrity" by proclaiming that "whatever their individual talents, teachers' unions and educrats have failed as a group to save the public schools. It's time to let someone else try" (1996, p. 40). The educational establishment's handling of change was characterized in this manner: "It's not really a wall—they always talk about change but rather more like quicksand, or a tar pit where ideas sink slowly out of sight, leaving everything just as it had been" (Alter, 1996, p. 40). Summit participants concluded that instead of the "usual educational fads," deep structural change must occur in standards, assessment, and accountability. One might criticize Alter's writing as an attempt to sensationalize a complex issue; however, his opinions are more likely to be read by the general public than are the reasoned debates in educational journals. This mélange of implied professional incompetence, genuine concern, and political jockeying creates a paralysis of will in educators as they engage the future.

As educators, the participants in this study were equally pessimistic; their acerbic comments reflect their experience with educational change:

> Barry: Change in education as I've seen it over thirty years is cyclic. It is trendy. It's faddish. It seems to go in four-five-six-year cycles where a certain type of education or certain approach to education is in favor. And, speaking for my school, we seem to jump on the bandwagon with whatever is most in favor. We grab on to it and ride it for a while, and it kind of fades. Then something new comes along, and we immediately shift gears and jump on the new bandwagon. Right now we're into block scheduling, which seems to be very good, but I'm sure if I were here long enough the block scheduling will be replaced with something new; just as block scheduling replaced other things.
>
> Sue: I guess in the whole scheme of things that there is an awful lot of repetition. It's sort of like fashion; things come in and go out. You wind up being able to see things being repeated. I remember when I was a student teacher and the big thing was behavioral objectives. You had to write everything in objective terms when doing the lesson plans, and then that kind of went away for a while. Then it got resurrected again during one of the fads that was going on in education, and now the objective way of dealing with things is couched in the terms of outcomes. A lot of times what is going on isn't all that different except for the terminology that is used.

Besides the cyclic repetitive nature of educational change, Sue also commented on the rapidity of change and the intervention of politics. Politics exacerbates the problems with educational change by disrupting the development of continuity in the implementation of a change initiative and in the reasoned assessment of the effectiveness of the change:

> Sue: And you know that sometimes I think that the reason why our heads are virtually spinning is because of the changes that come down [from the state]. We go through a writing curriculum change that we are only partially into, and then everything changes to outcome-based education. You know there is this thing about the state governor being perceived as anti-education by educators, so now we are going into this whole thing with outcomes wondering if he will be reelected? If he is, will all this stuff be thrown out? If not, what is going to come next?

Dave touched on two aspects of the problem with educational change: paper change versus real change and faddism. Dave's school recently implemented a portfolio assessment system to meet one of the state graduation requirements. In the plan, each of the curriculum departments would

Education in Crisis: The Postmodern Context   45

reinforce designated megaskills such as writing, speaking, organizing (that is, record keeping), problem solving, using technology, and visual communication:

Ray: Do you still do portfolios in your classroom?

Dave: I do because I believe in them. I'll do all of the things that we talked about. I do them at different times. My one project is based on that; it generates the whole project. So, yes, I think all of the ideas are really sound and really great. They should be in education, and they are not token [gestures]. So, yes, I do them, but I try not to mention the word portfolio to the kids because it turns them off.

Ray: To your knowledge, do a lot of other teachers still do portfolios?

Dave: To my knowledge—no. When I mention it they say, "You asshole, you still do that kind of thing?" So to them it is just a joke.

Ray: Well, on paper we have a portfolio system that is one of the best.

Dave: Right. For example a teacher in math will do one problem-solving model so that a kid has something to put in the portfolio, but they are not committed to the whole process. They don't do all the other items that should be included. The only thing that goes in the portfolio is really big-time token trash.

Ray: So in other words what is on paper isn't really the reality of the situation?

Dave: Nowhere near. Not even close. Yet the administration says that we do portfolios, but we all know that it isn't happening.

Ray: Let me run a few more changes by you that we have experienced over the years. Did the same thing happen to these that happened to portfolios? Erlene Minton [a proponent of Madeline Hunter's Effective Teaching program]?

Dave: Same thing. We were told to do these things, that they were to be implemented in our classroom, and then all of a sudden gone. You know fly-by-night, hit and miss.

Ray: Cooperative learning?

Dave: Same thing. We were in-serviced, and then there was no follow through. I do this one because I personally choose to do it, but I don't get to talk to anybody about refining it. You know it is kind of like smoke in the wind. Just blows away, comes and goes.

Ray: Critical thinking as in the use of graphic organizers?

Dave: They hit. They lasted for a little while, then they were carried away with the flood. They are gone, and no one ever mentions them again.

Ray: I was involved in the school district's multiple intelligence initiative. [At this point Dave started laughing.] How much have you been involved, and how much have you heard about this from the district?

Dave: I've read about it, I got some handouts, and I think one day we even talked about it during an in-service. But apply it to my class? I try to do different projects that address it, but I need more information, more feedback. I need more modeling, just as a football player would need that on the practice field, but it is like the coach walked away. There's nobody around anymore. The attitude is, "Okay, whatever you do is fine." That's what happens. I feel like I am on the playing field with my pants down.

One way in which the caustic commentary by these career teachers on their experience with change can be interpreted is within the context of modernism and the postmodern condition. Tony Wagner, in a study of three educational communities, argued that in understanding educational change "we need to begin with a redefinition of the educational 'problem.' Our schools have not somehow suddenly 'failed.' They have simply become obsolete" (1994, p. 249). Wagner supports this idea of educational obsolescence by identifying industrial-age, modernistic structures and processes that still maintain American schooling. He compares the administration/teacher-centered management strategies and the teacher-directed pedagogy to the need to develop students who can learn on their own and work effectively in teams. These last-mentioned skills are needed to efficiently function in the decentralized workplaces of the information age, instead of in the rigidly hierarchical workplace of an industrialized modern era characterized by its limited and limiting job classifications. Wagner's findings concerning schools can be readily applied to the postmodern situation in which today's families find themselves. Boundaries are blurred between the functions and responsibilities of adult and child, and with information as power, the child's access to power, especially in the context of popular culture, mediates the power differential between adult and child.

The change agendas and their accompanying processes are themselves obsolete. Portfolios become mere collection folders, and not new forms of assessment. Old structures of power and procedure are maintained in the intensive block schedule. Teachers dole out prescriptions that maintain modernistic roles, and hierarchies tightly control cooperative groups. Restructuring of curriculum resists the inclusion of the popular media that so essentially affect the meaning-making of the children. These examples represent the many faces of the old paradigm. The modernistic paradigm that controls education is a shape-shifter, a protean entity that takes on a variety of forms of change but always retains its true identity. The needs of a postmodern world cannot be met by the old paradigm; a new direction is required.

The Impact of Postmodernism on Educational Change
This perception that education is in a state of distress and impaired in its functioning is critically important in relation to the continuation of large-scale public education administered by educators. As society struggles with the postmodern condition, the educational community must present itself as the solution instead of as part of the problem. Being perceived as the solution will negate the insidious efforts of the conservative and com-

mercial interests who wish to minimize education or control it for purposes of self-interest. The task of the educational community is to determine why this situation of perceived failure exists and how it can be remedied.

David Elkind makes the interesting assertion that "the schools have already undergone a major transformation—independent of any conscious reform agenda simply in response to changes in the society and family" (1995, p. 14). Elkind contends that while education has been inertial in promoting relevant change, the postmodern family has been affecting the postmodern school.

Postmodernism is a contextual and philosophical problem that teachers and administrators must confront. The postmodern condition is characterized by hyperreality (the situation where "reality has collapsed, and today it is exclusively image, illusion, or simulation" [Rosenau, 1992, p. xi]) and hyperspace (a reference "to the fact that our modern concepts of space are meaningless" [Rosenau, 1992, p. xi], spatial barriers have disappeared and geography is in a flux, constantly shifting). Also, the old certainties that helped us distinguish between right and wrong are no longer unassailable. Logic, the objectivity and "rightness" of the expert, and the infallibility of science are challenged by emotion, intuition, and indigenous knowledge. As families move from place to place and the boundaries between the roles of parents and children become blurred, the old modernistic narratives about how families should operate no longer provide adequate answers. A pervasive relativism and situationality characterize the families and schools that are trying to center themselves, to establish a sustainable identity.

Andy Hargreaves further identifies this problem as involving an expansion of the teacher's role in taking on new problems and mandates without a change in the old role that will make room for these changes; an overload among educators due to the acceleration of change and the multitude of innovations; the crumbling of old missions and purposes; and the loss of educators' credibility due to the constant criticism of their methods (1994, p. 4). Also, the reality of a postmodern society is incongruent with "the hierarchical, bureaucratic decision-making structures that function in carefully defined, non-overlapping spheres" such as schools (Rosenau, 1992, p. 7).

The Purpose of Education
The acceleration of change and the crumbling of old missions and purposes mentioned by Hargreaves, as well as the postmodern family postulated by Elkind, surfaced in Sue's reflections on her purpose as a teacher:

> Obviously I am supposed to be educating kids, getting them ready, equipping them to face whatever it is that they are going to have to face when they leave school. But, I sometimes feel overwhelmed with what is going on in the world. There are so many changes going on so quickly. Kids are changing, their families are changing, and there are so many issues that they have to deal with that the kids have to be smarter quicker. I don't necessarily think that they are smarter, but they are exposed to so much more at such a younger age. They are in single-parent families, they have all kinds of technical equipment at home, and half of them are on the internet accessing who knows what. They are bombarded with unbelievable stuff in their music. We are seeing things in kids that we never saw before. We have these human beings who are bouncing off of the walls, who have been exposed to things at the age of fourteen that some adults have not seen in a lifetime.

Sue's comments suggest that the old, straightforward purpose of education, to "teach the kids," is now inadequate because of the hyperchange faced by the children of our times and the increasing complexity of their young lives.

Modernistic Professional Development

Another aspect of the problems generated by the interaction of the modern and the postmodern involves educational professional development. Educators are aware of the acceleration of change and the attributes and consequences of an information society, and they are aware that this condition has profound effects on their pedagogy. However, their professional development problems occur when modernistic models are used to deal with postmodern situations.

An example of these problems is seen in a description of an energetic and enthusiastic teacher's involvement in mathematics curriculum reform; the results included little change in her own instructional techniques, the failure of others to adopt new practices, and her cynicism concerning the success of future change initiatives (Wilson et al., 1996). Mrs. B, a highly successful teacher, entered into a three-year reform program designed to implement improvement in her mathematics teaching. The program focused on going beyond the basic instructional activities that dominated her curriculum to develop additional activities that would enhance student understanding. Mrs. B became a leader in her district's professional development by serving on its strategic planning committee and heading the professional development committee. She became proficient in new assessment procedures such as scoring rubrics and problem solving. However, after three years her teaching was not significantly different than before. This professional development effort culminated in a retention of basic skill instruction, a hesitation to use portfolios, and a skepticism about educational reform (Wilson et al., 1996). How could a motivated teacher engage in three years of professional development and not significantly change? Why are some teachers jaded and cynical regarding professional development?

Incompatible Out-Dated Beliefs

Part of the explanation for the pervasive cynicism of some educators, representing of varied years of experience, is the incompatibility of the teacher's belief structures with the postmodern context. Today's educators have never experienced what they are being required to do. They were taught in teacher-centered, knowledge-transmission-oriented classrooms whose sole purpose was the reproduction of the values and attitudes of those who dominated the culture of which they were a part. Their experience lies within this modernistic paradigm, and consequently they are unable to relate to the postmodern requirements of the contemporary situation. Aspects of the postmodern condition such as hyperchange, hyperreality, image saturation, and the fragmentation of reality contribute to the pluralistic, eclectic, and continuously changing nature of the contemporary classroom.

This incompatibility between what teachers believe about their purpose in relation to the postmodern condition surfaced in a group conversation. After Barry commented that society has gotten hung up on rights and has totally ignored the responsibilities of the individual, Steve made a comment that spoke to this incompatibility:

> Steve: You raised the question whether we are meeting the needs of society, and I think that we are meeting their needs. Society wants a place where they can put adolescents so they don't raise hell in the streets. That's a need that we achieve. Society wants us to keep them, feed them, make sure they are washed, and have at least one good meal. When you think about meeting the needs of society and look at what we are being asked to do, in a sense we are meeting those needs. The problem is, should they be the needs? Should this kind of thing be the function of school? That's the problem.
>
> Barry: You are saying that the needs that we are meeting are not academic needs?
>
> Steve: Well, yes. The function of school has changed in that it is out of control in the sense that our institution seems to be the only one left that can fulfill a lot of these needs. My bias is that these needs should not be the function of school. Our institution should serve the purpose of education and intellectual development.

Steve: Does society want this place to be a custodial institution to just hold students until they become part of the world of work? Do they want school to become a place where you develop your mind and intellect? Do they want this place to teach social skills on how people relate? Do they want this place to pass along the values of our society? So what are those core values, and how do we pass them along?

Barry: I don't think modern education meets anybody's needs. I don't think it meets the needs of the teachers, students, administrators, or society. Really, I don't think anybody is truly satisfied with modern education.

The personal educational experiences of these teachers imparted a different educational purpose than the aim that is required to meet the exigencies of the postmodern condition. The result of this incompatibility is confusion about societal needs, the purpose of education, and the role and behavior of teachers.

The older teachers and many of the younger ones were educated in schools during a period when the function of school was to transmit knowledge that would enable individuals to make the transition to the world of work or higher education. Their schools did not face all of the complex and diverse purposes facing current schools, such as facilitating high levels of intellectual development; preparing students for the workforce; providing mental health services; meeting basic nutritional and general health needs; and maintaining a safe environment. Their view of the purpose and function of schools is congruent with the purposes of the schools of their younger days, not with the postmodern context of today's public schools.

In a group conversation, after Steve expressed confidence in handling pedagogical changes within his area of control, a note of uncertainty crept into his reflection:

Steve: I do get the impression that based on everything that I have been through, in relation to pedagogy and method I can literally handle just about anything. So when we went to block scheduling I just kind of pictured how it should be. I find that I'm equipped from my own experiences to deal with just about any kind of thing that comes along. I feel that I could pretty much be in control of anything new that hits me. But on the other hand, there are things that I am experiencing now that deal with relationships with students and the way students are that I am not sure how to handle. I never thought that I would hear myself say that, but I think there is a distinct change in, not students as students, but students in their relationship to the whole social system. Students are different because society is different, and I don't feel equipped to handle this change.

Barry: You mean like a lack of standards and lowering standards?

Steve: Lowering standards in attitudes; you know attitudes, problems in this society that manifest themselves in school. And, I'm not talking about drugs, sex, and rock and roll. You know I'm talking about a general malaise in the attitudes about education and in the value of education. The change in attitudes is very distinct and shows up in behavior. These different values and attitudes affect what young people and their parents expect of school. We have to deal with these changes, and I'm not sure how to do that.

Besides their belief in standards as a solution, another incompatibility between these teachers' beliefs and the postmodern reality of their classrooms and their students was evident in the contrast between the complex needs of the students caught in a postmodern society and the teachers' beliefs that a large part of the problem with education lies in the unwillingness of the students to learn. This attitude could be simplistically construed as blaming the victim:

Steve: I just came out of a class exactly like that [where students do not take responsibility for their learning] so I'm a little frazzled because I literally had to tell these people what they had to make up, and they look at me like I am nuts. Sometimes I think that I am swimming upstream in trying to get them to have a sense of responsibility, to take ownership of their own lives. However, they are perfectly willing to be victims in the whole system. They don't realize that in my viewpoint public education is their only hope, their only chance to improve, to become something other than just a serf working in a mill.

Barry: I kind of think all the changes that we have incorporated over the thirty years that we have been here had the purpose of making the student feel more comfortable, gaining more self-esteem. We keep softening things so that the student has more self-esteem. We don't give a darn about the teacher's self-esteem. Everything's been incorporated to make life better for the student, and better doesn't necessarily mean more challenging. We have lowered our standards gradually over time. We want kids to feel good about themselves. Well, maybe they would feel good about themselves if they had some sort of knowledge when they walk out of here. They are going to leave feeling good about themselves and be totally void of academic knowledge.

Barry: What stops me from doing a better job is the kids' unwillingness to work. Just think what it would be like if the kids were really into learning. Just think of all the neat things you could do and the things you could teach them. I might never retire.

Ray: Could we do a better job of dealing with those kids who are disruptive all of the time, that hard core group? Could we do a better job meeting all of the kids' needs?

Barry: Yes.

Ray: How?
Barry: We need to eliminate those kids who serve as a detriment to the education of others. We need to eliminate those people who prevent others from obtaining a full education.
Ray: Okay, so you are basically saying expel a bunch of kids, and things will get better?
Barry: Well, it will be better. It won't be great, but it will be better.

The attitude that students are in control of their lives and therefore responsible for their behavior, along with the idea that expulsion is a viable solution to some of a school's problems, is indicative of modernistic thinking. A narrow view that focuses on one group of people ignores the overwhelming complexity of a school system. The problems with a reductionist view is that systemic, holistic solutions are not possible. Whether expulsions or the latest fad, quick fixes are the norm instead of reasoned, moral design. The rigid structure and imperviability to change of educational systems limit the solutions to the real problems identified by these teachers. If the school day, the number of teachers, the roles of stakeholders in the system, the curriculum and instruction, and the amount of available money are not negotiable, how can any other options be discussed? In a rigid modernistic system, draconian measures like expulsion are viable options for maintaining the status quo.

Universality, the Specter of Relativism and the Dominance of the Expert

Beyond the incompatibility of teacher beliefs and the solutions required for the postmodern condition, postmodernism also impacts education in the demise of universality and the specter of relativism. Postmodernism contends that there are no universal truths. "What works in one situation doesn't work in another" (Guskey & Huberman, 1995, p. 117). The answers must come from the participants, therefore, answers will be different from school to school. The individual or group can no longer look to the horizon of universality, universalization, or general emancipation (Lyotard, 1993) for instruction on how to navigate the currents of change. The segue of educational changes reported by the participants consisted of change initiatives developed outside of their school. These well-planned packages of educational wisdom were promoted as panaceas for all schools. These professional development initiatives were modernistic in assuming that an outside expert could craft a plan that would be relevant to many different educational systems and could be effectively implemented in the traditional, top-down manner. Were these supposed panaceas appropriate for the participants' school? Apparently they were not. Part of the problem is that information overload, unfamiliar forms and content of discourse, and unfamiliar critical language all contribute to the frustration of professional development efforts.

When engaged in this deconstructing process of postmodern discourse, the individual teacher or group is simultaneously decentering from established metanarratives and from the possibility of constructing new ones that are germane to their local context. Patti Lather (1986) sees this decentering not so much as an elimination of the established narrative but as a reconceptualization of the narrative as multicentered with a plurality of meaning. To accomplish this shift, individuals must converse. Through conversation, language is used to create personal meaning, which leads to the construction of narratives that support collegial cultures imbued with moral purpose. However, conversation that includes teacher input in policy-making issues and discusses the critical reflections of teachers rarely occurs. The outcome of this lack of conversation is a continuation of the old narratives that are no longer relevant to a postmodern situation, as seen in the conversation about expulsion and about students as the primary agents in controlling their own lives.

Besides the enervating relativism, the role of the educational expert in professional development is problematic. Postmodern literature decries the cult of expertise (Pinar et al., 1995). Gary Sykes points out that the one-shot workshop "supports a mini-industry of consultants without having much effect on what goes on in schools and classrooms" (1996, p. 465). Joe Kincheloe reports that "teachers with weak academic, theoretical, and pedagogical backgrounds must defer to the judgments of educational leaders, the certified experts" (1993, p. 183). When expertism controls professional development, teachers are involved only as passive recipients of the current dogma; they are empowered only to the extent authorized by the expert. The type of conversation allowed by the expert is dialogic only if it promotes the expert's agenda; otherwise the expert creates a dialectical conversation by resorting to strong technical arguments to win the point. Teachers are not seen as experts, and their lack of inclusion in the change process is seminal in an understanding of educational change.

In a postmodern context, Mrs. B engaged change on a superficial level and in a reductionist manner. Rubrics, problem-solving strategies, portfolios, and other assessment and instructional strategies are surface phenomena that mask the deeper, hidden forces whose resolution determines the outcome of change. The reduction of the educational environment to specific components, like rubrics and portfolios, distracts the change agent from a critical reflection on deeper concerns such as past practice, future goals, student and parent ownership in the change process, the study of theory and its relationship to practice, the peculiarities and eccentricities of the place where the change would occur, the systemic effects of the change (for example, beyond the teacher's classroom; on the teacher's life) on the meanings that the teacher has constructed about education. Mrs. B was ensnared in the current modernistic professional development process characterized by expertism. Instead of broadening her intuition and knowledge through critical reflection, she followed the in-service path established by the experts, and she eventually became an expert. Despite this accomplishment, her achievements seemed empty and devoid of authenticity and relevance to her students and herself. Through her energy, dedication, and determination Mrs. B proved that she was a capable and motivated professional. However, the modernist path of change led to a dissatisfaction and resentment that could harden into a cynical skepticism about all change initiatives.

Autobiographical Reflection

The impact of postmodernism on educational change can best be seen in the roles of expertism, reductionism, and autobiographical reflection inherent in the professional development experienced by teachers. The case has been made that modernistic professional development, which is the norm, is typically teeming with experts and is reductionist in its focus. It is also typical for teachers to reflect only rarely on their autobiographical stories. Yet the very nature of the postmodern condition of education requires a holistic approach, the egalitarian involvement of all stakeholders, and the inclusion, not denigration, of the experiential and intuitive knowledge of all stakeholders.

Individual and collective autobiographical reflection and the concurrent interpretations of those reflections are the lifeblood of authentic problem solving and of a moral commitment to a shared vision. Solving the problems posed by the postmodern condition requires community building, which, in turn, requires the development of trust. Shared reflection of an autobiographical and psychoanalytic nature creates that trust.

In a group conversation, some of the participants in this study recognized the value of autobiographical reflection:

> Dan: I think the thing that stood out the most to me is that I was forcing myself to look back and see the different things that we did over the years. I realized that we were in a situation where we had experiences that many

teachers never go through. Just the experience of having closed classrooms, then going to open classrooms, then going back to closed classrooms. It was an experience that few people would go through in their career.

Barry: You know, I think that is really a good point. The combined experiences that we have sitting at this table are really kind of amazing because we have experienced the full gamut of educational trends and fads. Few teachers have had the experiences that we have had.

Steve: From that perspective since we have been part of a lot of changes, I think that we also get a particularly interesting perspective on why things don't work—why they failed. You have a chance to look at the big picture over the long haul. You know you have a kind of continuum that you can look back on and say, "I know why this didn't work, or why this could have worked, but this was the problem." It is almost like we have been part of an on-going experiment.

Fixing the complex problems of a postmodern society is a complicated proposition, and maybe the idea that they can be fixed (suggesting permanence) is itself part of the problem. Maybe educators need to build a reservoir of experience that can be used to inform the theory that they deem relevant to their local system. Of course, that experience must be recalled and critically reflected upon in the context of the theory. But when will this occur? Does the system and culture of the school accommodate or resist this source of solutions?

A Cultural Crisis

Teacher Culture

The importance of culture in educational reform is ubiquitous in the professional literature. Andy Hargreaves (1994) reports that various cultures of teaching impact the effectiveness of professional development and consequently of change. He delineates culture in terms of its content and form. Content indicates attitudes, beliefs, habits, and the way things are done. Form deals with the patterns of relationships and associations between the teacher and other members of the culture. According to Hargreaves, form has the greater implications for educational change. Four forms of culture are identified: individualism, collaboration, contrived collegiality, and balkanization. Individualism and balkanization are forms of modernistic culture, with contrived collegiality a superficial modernistic response aimed at offsetting the deleterious aspects of individualism and balkanization.

Collaboration is often offered as the panacea for the postmodern problems of educational change. However, to be effective in facilitating change collaboration must be viewed in the broader context of power relationships and the types of conversation that occur between the members of the culture when collaborating. Without this contextualization, determining whether a collaboration is authentic or contrived is difficult. For example, mandated collaboration that employs dialectical or other means of controlling conversation leads to a contrived collegiality that is administratively regulated, compulsory, implementation oriented, and fixed in time. Since teachers' time is highly contextualized, this administrative attempt to standardize teachers' work and time leads to inflexibility and inefficiency in the implementation of change (Hargreaves, 1994).

If collaboration is not systemically utilized throughout the whole school, balkanization occurs. Balkanization is a form of teacher culture in which teachers form significant relationships with others in smaller subgroups within the community. These departments, units, divisions, or cliques act as a lens that focuses the individual's loyalty and commitment. This form of culture is problematic for effective change because it blocks total community interaction and cohesion by insulating the subgroups, promoting political activity between the sub-groups, and fostering identification with the subgroup instead of with the school culture. This cultural form can be further debilitating when it occurs within departments as well as between them (Hargreaves, 1994).

The power relationships between individuals and groups in a school culture contribute to the success or failure of change. Teacher cultures characterized by individualism, contrived collegiality, and balkanization (Hargreaves, 1994) support modernistic, hierarchical, and hegemonic educational systems that resist change. A school of individuals isolated in separate classrooms will be a school with a multitude of individual agendas that fail to coalesce into a collective vision. Change initiatives will be short-lived because no one person or group will have the power to establish an idea. Change attempts in balkanized schools will likewise be short-lived because each department or group will assiduously work to promote its own ideas and welfare. The dialectical and adversarial nature of the interactions will once again doom any chance for an authentic collective vision. Contrived collegiality is an administrative tool that, because of its very nature, fails to create significant change. Contrived collegiality fails to develop relevant, authentic change because it is administratively regulated, compulsory, implementation oriented, fixed in time and space, and predictable (Hargreaves, 1994).

In addition, any benefits from positive teacher actions will be contained within the small sphere of influence of the individual teacher or that teacher's department. In balkanized, individualized, and contrived teacher cultures, no one person or group has sufficient power to effect system-wide change. This limited influence, coupled with the natural resistance to change found within systems, dooms any possibility of substantial change.

One theme that constantly reoccurred in the conversation with all the participants was a comparison of teacher culture between the late 1980s and 1990s and the 1970s and early 1980s. This theme reflected the effect of balkanization on the moral commitment of the teachers. Initially, Barry talked about this difference in general terms. After theory regarding teacher culture was introduced, Barry became very specific:

Ray: Let us continue talking about the school system, but this time let's focus on the culture of the school. In my feedback that I gave you after our first interview, I identified different types of school culture. Do you see any elements of that in our situation?

Barry: Most definitely, in that balkanization has occurred gradually over the last nine years. We have gone from the open space where people communicated freely to a closed classroom type of situation where each department is in a specific area and there is very little intermingling of departments. We have been balkanized.

Ray: Another type of culture was called contrived collegiality. You chuckle, so I guess you remember what that means.

Barry: Well, I don't really remember, but if anything is contrived then it has to be occurring here.

Ray: Well, as I interpreted Hargreaves's work, it is when you have relationships that are administratively regulated. They are not spontaneous; meetings are compulsory. The focus is on implementing the mandates of others, and the encounters between teachers take place at particular times and places as determined by the administration.

Barry: That is basically the way we restructured the high school.

Ray: Do you see any problems or benefits with that?

Barry: Personally, I had major problems with that because there was no input from the faculty. It was structured from the top down. Teachers were assigned to different committees whether they were interested or not. Excessive meetings were held that angered most people, but they attended because they didn't have the courage not to attend. The committees functioned without any decision-making power. Most of the decisions, and by most I mean 95 percent, were pre-made. The only ones that were left to the teachers were the decisions that the people in charge didn't have the ability to make themselves. So, therefore, they had to call a committee in order to make those decisions. There still is no ownership in any of these committees. Most people are just on a committee, and grin and bear it.

Ray: The other one was collaborative or collegial. In this culture you have working relationships between teachers that are spontaneous. In other words, it means when there is a need, you talk. The relationships are voluntary, and the people are focused on developing initiatives of their own. Change comes out of the discussion that teachers have about their environment.

Barry: That's the way we did things in the old days.

Ray: In the old days?

Barry: Right! That's the 1970s, when we did things not because they were fads but because they were needed or because the times called for it—because they were necessary. It might have grown out of a faculty-room conversation, a department meeting, a general faculty meeting, or just casual discussion among professionals. Those things don't happen any more.

Later in the conversation, I asked Barry to clarify who the "people" in his comment that people during the 1970s were motivated to have relationships. I asked if he was referring only to his English department.

Barry: No, they were just people; not departments. The division that exists today didn't exist back then. We have become departmentalized today, where we are either the English department or the social studies department. In the 1970s we were just faculty, and we developed bonds.

I later commented on individualization within a department, pointing out in that we in the social studies department used to consider ourselves tightly knit, but since the demise of the open classroom we have become individualized. Barry offered:

I think that happened in the English department. In the open area we used to converse a lot and share ideas, make suggestions, and interact with each other. This no longer occurs because of the change in structure [the change to self-contained classrooms].

Sue and Dan further described the balkanization of the faculty. Sue's comments were reactions to the theory on teacher culture and postmodernism that I introduced after her first interview, while Dan's comments were in response to a question about how often he interacted with other teachers:

Sue: It looks like we are becoming destined to fail as educators. Is that possible? How can teachers succeed when we don't even know where we are going? Another thing is the balkanization of teachers. Instructional planning centers [IPCs; in the restructured building, each department has a room containing a planning station for each teacher] completely balkanize us. Why do they do that? Are the administrators familiar with theory like this, or is there a game plan to try to separate teachers—to isolate teachers; because IPCs do exactly that. They have replaced faculty rooms, and therefore the whole notion of having teachers being able to communicate and do anything collegial is eliminated by the physical plant.

Dan: Now with the teachers I think we need to have a sharing of ideas. I think one of the biggest mistakes in block scheduling is the fact that social studies and English aren't in the same semester. [This means that a student does not have these two courses during the same semester; a possible pairing would be English and science or math and social studies. During a semester a student studies only two major subjects.] My best class is the one that developed from sitting down with one of the social studies teachers and figuring out how to coordinate the literature with what was being taught in Advanced Placement American History. I think that exchange of ideas is important, and that is what I liked about the mini-courses. [This is a reference to the mini-courses that were created from the English/social studies interdisciplinary teaming in the ITSS program described in Chapter One.] A drawback of the block schedule is that I don't have as many opportunities to find out what is going on in other areas, because I only get a chance to see and interact with the people that are in my planning period.

Ray: Do you think that having an opportunity to talk with colleagues is a factor in the success or failure of a change?

Dan: Yes, I think it is definitely a factor, and that it is something that I hope we don't sacrifice. That is why I would personally like to see things changed next year so that there would be times that several of the social studies teachers, several of the English teachers, math, science, art, and music teachers could get together. I don't know the answer in how to schedule it, but I think this should be taken into consideration in building the schedule so that there would be common times where you can get some new ideas.

Dave had a more political view on the balkanization and individualization that is characteristic of this school's culture:

Dave: Absolutely no value comes from the in-service organized by outsiders, and the best happens when we meet in our department, when we meet with other teachers. One year we met with the English department to coordinate the writing. That was really good, but again that was dangerous [Dave's view of how the administration would perceive such meetings]. When do we have the time to observe other classrooms or meet with other teachers? We don't.

Ray: What you just talked about as far as professional development, and not having time to meet with others; is this how it always has been for you?

Dave: Always. When we do get together they [the administration] look at it as down time as opposed to productive time. I guess they feel threatened by that time because it goes out of their control. The fact that our communication is controlled is how it is in a dictatorship. If I don't want a rebellion, I don't let people get together to talk. I keep them apart. That is the strategy of any dictatorial system. You don't allow people to communicate. So if I were an administrator who would take a democratic approach, I would say that the teachers have the power to govern and to control what they do. I am the leader, and I feel confident in that; so I then back off and let them meet. In fact I would facilitate their meeting. I wish education would be democratic. If you [administrators] always had a history of dictatorship, it is very difficult to break this habit and go in another way. It is very fearful for people in charge to move away from that state.

In sum, the teachers described the balkanized and individualized culture of this school as having a deleterious effect on teacher relationships as well as on the promotion of change. The requirements of the postmodern condition, the school culture, and the efficacy of educational change must be viewed holistically because they are dynamically interrelated.

Inclusion of Student Cultures

The inclusion of all the community's stakeholders means the inclusion of the students in decision making. The modernistic paradigm, in its characteristic manifestation as hierarchical, centralized, bureaucratic, and educator centered, does not recognize student culture as a critical ingredient in the change process, and, therefore, it excludes students from the covenant. Yet students are stakeholders, and their inclusion in the change process requires an appraisal of their culture. Central to this appraisal is the realization that student culture is a composite of student-generated culture, culture as transmitted by the dominant culture, culture generated by popular media, and culture resulting from commodification by commercial interests (Giroux, 1994; Steinberg & Kincheloe, eds., 1997). The recognition of students as stakeholders requires educators to be cognizant of popular culture and its manipulation by commercial interests.

Postmodern problems require the school culture to develop spaces that will allow students to articulate their particular cultures within the larger school culture. The inclusion of students as colleagues in learning and partners in the change process will be achieved by replacing the current pedagogies of cordiality, which strive to maintain hegemonic control while maintaining a congenial relationship between the educators and the students (Giroux, 1988), with collaborative and egalitarian pedagogies that include students as decision makers in educational change.

When asked if she ever thought of using popular culture through media as the catalyst for writing activities, Sue replied:

> I haven't done that. Popular culture comes up when they make references to movies or television, and when they use examples of TV or movie characters to defend a point of view. I haven't done that [used popular culture to promote relevance and authenticity], and part of the problem that I have is that I am not

familiar with popular culture. It's not part of my life, and to use it is like stepping into grounds in which I have no knowledge base. Pretty much I don't watch television, and so I don't know what they are watching and what is out there.

Empowering students is as much about learning about the culture that directly affects their attitudes and behaviors as it is about giving them power. In postmodern theory, the complementary ideas of collegial collaboration, moral leadership, and the inclusion of all stakeholders work together to create powerful school cultures that can lead to the improvement of education for our children. However, the inclusion of all stakeholders means inclusion of students in decisions that affect them, collegial collaboration means replacing the hierarchical dominance of adults over students with the same collegiality that should exemplify adult professional relationships, and moral leadership means providing reflective and learning opportunities for students to develop the same moral commitment to a community that should typify adult professional communities.

None of this can happen if the adults who interact with students do not have a working knowledge of the student culture and the larger popular culture that so greatly informs student attitudes and behaviors. Strategies that create the possibility of a new direction leading to collaboration, moral commitment, and inclusion make it possible to find solutions to the postmodern problems of education.

A Spiritual Crisis

In reflecting upon my prior experience as described in the introduction and Chapter One, I became aware of one distinct difference between my experiences in the 1970s and 1980s and my later experience in the 1990s. This is spirituality, more specifically an animating or vital principle that gave life to my professional efforts. Spirituality in this sense does not mean sacred or religious, but it includes the transcendent and motivational qualities of the sacred. In the early years, my perception was that I was part of something greater than myself, connected to a community, and, therefore, motivated to make an extraordinary effort to promote my community's values and vision. Somewhere in the 1980s, this sense of the spiritual was lost.

Barry alluded to what we termed spirituality in relation to the years prior to the 1980s:

> I talked to Dave yesterday, and he again expressed the interest in reading other people's comments. I would love to do that, and he and I talked about a culminating roundtable discussion for all the participants to get together and kind of draw a closing to this activity. Your use of the word spirituality really brought up something to me. As we look at the 1970s, it is almost a spiritual experience because there are so many emotional things that you can draw from that time. When you look at the past, there was a common bonding. There was almost a spiritual experience in that I think of people who participated in that time period who still hold those bonds. As we said before there was a uniting of people; of spirits, back

at that time. We were individuals but yet we were, for better or for worse, a group who held common ideas, values, motivations, desires, and wishes. We were in many ways one. So, yes, I would be interested in sharing. I would like to see a roundtable, or whatever pleases the other participants.

When studying postmodernity's efforts to restore theology and spirituality to the curriculum discourses and practices of the 1990s (Slattery, 1995), I came to an intuitive agreement with this restoration. Additionally, when I revisited the early years and the recent past, it became clear to me that the essential element we have all missed in recent years is the motivational spirituality that is inherent in a collegial community. The importance of this phenomenon became apparent in the participants' repeated commentary on the camaraderie, collegiality, sociability, and the collective professional vision toward which we strived. Simply put, we have missed that sort of connectedness and stimulation.

Martin Buber's Intersubjectivity and Spirituality

A study of Martin Buber contextualized the transcendent nature of my early experience. Buber (1992) is concerned with the nature of the interpersonal, which he saw as the core of social relations. He distinguishes between an I-Thou and an I-It relationship between two people (1988). The I-Thou relationship is one of immediacy and intimacy, while the I-It relationship is one of objectification and instrumentality. Buber asserts that both relationships are evident and purposeful in society; however, the significant question is "whether the I-Thou relation remains the architect" (1988, p. 128).

Buber maintains that societies in which the I-It relation is pervasive are societies and cultures in a state of stagnation. The vitality of creatively energized societies and cultures arises because of the generative aspects of the interpersonal relations of the stakeholders who "are united in a symmetrical bond that maintains their individualities but brings them into living relation with each other" (Buber, 1988, p. xii). This interpersonal interaction results in spiritual understandings about others and subsequently the issues characterized by Buber as "revelations." However, to achieve this state of being, individuals must recognize the spontaneity of these occurrences, and be in a state of readiness to receive them. The state of readiness is achieved in dialogic conversation, which occurs best in collegial and collaborative cultures.

The consensus of the participants and myself is that our earlier experiences were more indicative of I-Thou than I-It relationships. A state of constant readiness existed, due to the collaborative and collegial teacher culture, the sense of personal ownership in the change process, the provision of opportunities within the school day for dialogical conversation, and later the spatial accommodation of these conditions fostered by the open-space facility.

Buber insists that "nothing no possible insight, report, or knowledge at all—can substitute for confronting an other directly and immediately. Experiences, events, relations can be described and analyzed, but description, no matter how vivid, and analysis, no matter how acute, cannot serve as alternatives for responsiveness, 'here and now'" (Buber, 1988, p. xi). Understanding the continuously changing nature of situations and people requires continuous interaction, not only because the "It" and the "Thou" change, but also because the "I" is in a state of continuous change. To maintain I-Thou relationships in an educational setting it is necessary to provide space and opportunity for ongoing dialogic and design conversation. Such conversation is the main factor in maintaining shared visions and group identity. To enhance the moral aspect of community building, dialogical conversation needs to occur more frequently than conversation of a more observational and objective nature. In the earlier years, as people and situations changed, the sense of collegial community and the social and professional opportunities for conversation allowed us to stay in touch with each other professionally and personally.

Buber recognizes the ideological and emotional differences that arise in dialogic conversation. Buber depicts these differences as being in a state of constant reciprocity and tension in dialogic conversation. In a sense, tension is a safeguard against homogeneity, a mechanism to challenge prior assumptions in a dialogically and I-Thou enhancing context. Buber cautions that without the state of tension between autonomous groups in a society, "the domination of any one element over the others, and the potential annihilation of any such element by others, may produce just routine organizational or structural change, or it may lead to the stagnation, or even to the demise, of a society or culture" (1992, p. 11).

The participants agreed that a significant factor in the dissolving of the early communal and spiritual quality of our collective commitment was the change in administrative attitudes toward teacher empowerment. The administration of the 1980s and 1990s reestablished a traditional hierarchy with policy decision making firmly in its own hands. Also, with the renovation of the school, the advent of the self-contained classroom greatly facilitated administrative control by reinforcing an already balkanized and individualized teacher culture. It would be simplistic to conclude that the outcome was a stagnant school culture. However, the collective spiritualism that permeated prior change efforts was no longer evident.

In the cultures of isolation (balkanized and individualized) that pervade many public schools, the routinized professional development that further objectifies all stakeholders, the denial of the spirit, the ignorance of the systemic nature of schools, and the lack of critical contextualization have become factors in the failure of educational reform.

Learning Organizations and Shared Vision

How does a school facilitate the development of the essential animating principles indicative of a transcendent community (that is, common vision, spiritual commitment, I-Thou relationships, caring)? Peter Senge is a systems theorist who proposes that the best way to deal with change is through a learning organization. A learning organization to Senge is not an organization with a destination but an organization constantly involved in "study and practice." A successful learning organization must "penetrate to deep changes in culture and traditional practices" with people "working on themselves while they are working on 'their system'" (Senge, 1990, p. xvii). This need for deep change can be achieved through postformal conversation (which will be discussed in Chapter Four). Senge's vision of a learning organization is relevant to an understanding of how schools could pursue the new direction that is presented in Chapter Four.

Vision is a critical part of Senge's learning organization. Unlike the current working definitions of visions in educational organizations, Senge's shared vision and Sergiovanni's moral leadership and followership (1992) clearly show the power of individual and collective human activity within systems. Current visions and mission statements are ideas that embellish letterheads, that are developed by selected individuals, and that are not remembered by anyone in the organization. Senge's shared vision is not an idea but rather a palpable force of impressive power in people's hearts. A large part of the strength of Senge's vision is that it is shared but still encompasses personal visions. This is not a normal occurrence in the top-down visions developed by a few administrators and select groups of other stakeholders. Shared visions do not require people to "buy in" to the vision; people participate in the construction of the vision. Organizations guided by shared visions do not experience conditions of "malicious obedience" or include stakeholders who are "grudgingly compliant" (Senge, 1990, p. 220). The processes that facilitate the development of a shared vision (that is, critical reflective thinking, post-formal conversation, praxis) facilitate the stakeholders' ability to work through the diversity of views, conflicting visions, polarization, discouragement, and proselytizing that derail many well-intentioned vision-building efforts. Senge argues that the problem with shared vision building lies "in our reactive orientation toward current reality. Vision becomes a living force only when people truly believe they can shape their future" (1990, p. 231).

The participants in the research project recognized that the early years were more indicative of a learning organization than the recent years. The collegial culture that existed in the 1970s fostered a shared vision of education and professional collaboration. At one point, Barry and I were talking about the professional dialogue that took place during the 1970s and the fact that is was not restricted to the school environment but took place elsewhere, especially at social functions.

> Barry: I think those kind of things [social functions] build collegiality. Collegiality is what you need. You need a cohesive group working together for a common goal, not five different groups working together for that goal.
> Ray: In systems thinking they call what you just said, about a common goal, a vision. A vision is a little more than a goal; it is also a dream. It is a coming together with a common dream about how things should be, and then trying to design a system that will allow the achievement of your dream. Do you think there was a vision in the 1970s?
> Barry: Yes, because I think everybody was coming from a commonality of perspective, of desires for the future. Again we were a group that had common goals, common desires, common aims, common rules. We shared everything in common. It was a singular vision, a singular view. Today the view is disjointed. There isn't any commonality; there are many divergent visions. The common vision doesn't exist.

Sue had a definite opinion about the existence of a learning organization in the early years.

> The early years were definitely indicative of a learning organization. The collegial climate was one that fostered teaching and teachers as evolving because of the motivational carrot of doing better. Perhaps the carrot has changed from betterment to survival, and that is not good. A lack of collegiality results in a "feel-your-way" approach to teaching rather than a "lead-the-way" reciprocity that many of us experienced in the open classroom. I had wonderful and varied teaching models—Habe, Barry, Dan, and Carolyn, all of whom were valuable to me in a variety of ways. Most importantly, I had feedback.

Roldan Tomasz Suarez critiqued Senge's ideas in an inquiry into the historical meaning of Senge's "Fifth Discipline." One of Surarez's conclusions is that "the modern experience of humanity is vanishing in our culture and we are beginning to recognize ourselves in a different humanity" (1998, p. 501). He concludes his critique with a question: "To what degree can organizations become the preeminent space for an authentic reappearance of a human being engaged with the whole?" (p. 501). The comments of Barry and Sue indicate at least a perceived engagement with the whole in the earlier years of the open-space environment. Decidedly, their current assessment of their position in the school is one of benign disengagement that, at best, has resulted in an instrumental accommodation with the other stakeholders, specifically the administration. There appears to be a paucity of spaces that would enable their reapproachment with the whole. Is the situation in this school, as perceived by these teachers, the result of the failure of the modern experience of humanity to accommodate itself to the exigent conditions of our postmodern society? What then must change, to create these spaces that will generate an inclusive community culture that can realistically deal with the problems of postmodernity? The answer to this question does not lie with the continued application of modernistic strategies but in the potential of ideas such as Senge's.

Answering the Critics and Resolving the Crises

The task of answering the critics and resolving the crises of education is a difficult one. However, one step in providing an answer is the formulation of a new direction. A review of the literature on educational change and the findings of this research indicate that certain ideas and attitudes must be part of a new direction. A new direction would have to contain ideas and attitudes that are synergistically interrelated, in that together they actively create an energy and a condition that is greater than any of the ideas and attitudes as separate entities.

The formation of a community would be essential but it must be more than just a community, a transcendent community imbued with the spiritual commitment to a shared vision. Equally important is the culture of the community. Does the culture facilitate the construction of a transcendent community, or is it counterproductive? Is there a collective awareness of the importance of a systemic view that broadens the community's awareness of its place in the larger environment? Are members of the community aware of the interactive process of meaning-making and the concomitant effect of affect on the construction of meaning?

The exigencies of the postmodern condition require a critical examination of school cultures, the role of spirituality in educational change, and the type of organizations that can readily accommodate the postmodern condition. The new direction that will now be presented must be contextualized within the framework of collegial cultures, new administrative cultures that empower all stakeholders and blur the boundaries between the current hierarchical levels, the inclusion of student cultures in the curriculum and instruction, the development of an I-Thou spiritual commitment to the school community, and the establishment of learning organizations characterized by shared visions.

The most important ingredient in this mixture is the understanding of the role of conversation in community building and in the quest for the vision. Post-formal conversation is the essential, ubiquitous mechanism, the primary process in all human activity. A new direction must set aside spaces for post-formal conversation within the community's daily routine. All of these ideas constitute the new direction.

Chapter Four

A New Direction

If education is to meet the demands of a postmodern society, we must put aside the modernistic paradigm and move in a new direction. Even the reform focus on progress is problematic. There seems to be an essential American optimism that things will somehow always work out. Somehow, someone will keep us moving forward, progressing to a better state. New standards will be formulated and generalized to all of the schools. Somehow the rigors of the scientific method will allow us to persevere as we have before. This thinking is part of the modernistic mythology justifying the reform actions that continue to fail. Continuing to base change on the old paradigm does not lead to progress but to continuous failure to meet the needs of our society. Optimism and progress only become effectively operational in the postmodern context if they are based upon the synergetic components of this new direction.

Society appears to be in one of Thomas Kuhn's paradigm shifts (1996), a transitional period in which the old way of doing business is inadequate in the face of the enormous changes in our social and physical environment. Peter H. Wagschal recognizes that "the course schooling follows in the coming decades will depend on the paradigms people adopt in adjusting to a rapidly changing world" (1994, p. 51). He characterizes people's paradigms as "both their greatest assets and their most paralyzing handicaps and they can blind people to possibilities that go unheard despite their deafening roar" (p. 52). Personal and societal survival creates the imperative that action must be taken to initiate these requisite paradigm shifts in the most important enculturating medium, education.

To create a school system that is relevant to a postmodern society, the current school structure must be dismantled and replaced by a democratic system with institutional characteristics such as shared ownership, systemic thinking, an egalitarian culture, recognition of moral responsibility, spiritual commitment, and post-formal conversation.

The narrative presented in Chapter One told of a modernistic school district that consistently failed in its change initiatives due to the lack of sustainable collegial cultures, spiritual commitment, and learning organization. Whatever the change initiative was, some stakeholder groups were always excluded from the decision making or limited in their participation. The educators failed to take the systemic view and connect their immediate context with those of other subsystems and suprasystems. School culture was balkanized as each department represented its own interests and resisted integration with other segments of the school culture. Departmental and individual self-interest dominated the decision-making process. The nascent spiritual commitment to community building was still born due to the replacement of collegial and design forms of conversation with oppositional conversational forms such as dialectic and discussion. The change situation explicated in the narrative is typical of public schools entrenched in the modernistic paradigm.

To move beyond the modernistic paradigm would require a foundational recognition of the individual and the individual's interaction with others in the social constructions of reality. The motivation to include and empower people, to value their knowledge and input, is based upon the realization that people interpret situations in their own way and are affected by the interpretations of others. In addition, there is an emotional or affective component in these interactive constructions that directly affects individual motivation to resist or accommodate change.

Recognition of this critically constructivistic viewpoint must be embedded in a qualitative epistemological framework that, through post-formal conversation, facilitates the development of an egalitarian community that is a learning organization.

The Significance of Conversation

All change, reform, or progress must start with conversation. The status quo can be changed when conversation occurs. Metaphorically, the moment of conversation is like the moment of measurement for Schrödinger's cat (Gribbin, 1995). This classic conundrum in quantum physics shows that the act of measurement (in this case merely opening the box to see if the cat is dead or alive) is implicated in the outcome of the event. While hidden in the box, Schrödinger's cat is both dead and alive. This reality is maintained until the experimenter opens the box. At this point, reality becomes tangible or defined. As in the case of Schrödinger's cat, all possibilities and potentials related to a change initiative are possible until conversation occurs. When conversation occurs, forces affecting change are activated, and they become agents attempting to influence the outcomes of the conversation.

When a school remains in stasis (the cat in the box), all realities are mere potentials. Beginning a conversation is like opening the box. In a balkanized school, when conversation occurs that allows mindsets to be temporarily set aside, a process is started that can lead to extraordinary outcomes involving egalitarian and collegial action. Conversation creates the potential for commonality in visions and the more efficient achievement of individual and group goals. On the other hand, the control of conversation by one group maintains the culture that they dictate.

How people converse and who controls the conversation is an often-overlooked component in the change process. All stakeholders in a school need to engage in conversation about theory and practice, their professional and local cultures, the dispersion and judicious uses of power, and the development and reinforcement of their individual and collective moral commitments to educational change. Out of conversations of this nature comes the spirituality inherent in shared visions. The effectiveness of conversation in realizing successful change is directly related to the type of conversation. Some types will be counterproductive, some collegially generative. Dialogic conversation is one essential element of post-formal conversation, which, in turn, is foundational to a new direction.

Types of Conversation

Patrick Jenlink and Alison Carr (1996) present a continuum of four types of conversation: dialectic, discussion, dialogue, and design. Dialectic and discussion are probably the most frequently occurring types. They are characterized by logical, disciplined argument used to promote ideologies and beliefs, invariably resulting in the polarization or alienation of the group. People who engage in dialectical conversation "are threatened by anyone who thinks differently from them, and so regard it as their responsibility to convert others to their view. Members have a clash of personally held beliefs and assumptions. Members, instead of accepting one another, try to 'fix one another'" (Avers et al., 1996, p. 32). On the other hand, dialogue and design facilitate the development of a "oneness," a shared culture sustained by morally committed people. In dialogue, people examine their personal assumptions and then suspend them, thus opening new spaces where new meanings can be constructed. Dialogue requires a respect for other views and a recognition that the intended outcome is the development of community.

The distinction between dialogue and design is that in design conversation people focus on creating something new. When engaged in creating change through design conversation, the participants are committed "to change *of* the system rather than change *within* the system" (Jenlink & Carr, 1996, p. 35). In dialogue, the participants "focus on building a conscious collective mindfulness of community that creates a common sense of purpose and shared vision" (Jenlink & Carr, 1996, p. 35). In the context of current restructuring efforts, design conversation would lead to something new; not just a reshuffling of a school schedule and minor changes in curriculum and instruction to accommodate mandated change but a new concept of curriculum, instruction, and administration.

Another way to understand design is to compare it to the current restructuring efforts. Bela H. Banathy explains this difference as form following function:

> In restructuring we attempt to correct for the wrongs by changing relations among the parts, by redefining the role played by people in the system, or redefining the role of the components of the system. Having done so, we find that the boundaries of the system have not changed; neither have we changed purposes and functions. Restructuring might bring about change within the system, but it does not create a new system. Designers, on the other hand, focus on creating a new image of the system, define the purpose based on the image, and select the functions that attend to the purpose. (1996b, p. 21)

Dialogic Conversation

The significance of dialogic conversation as a component of the new direction requires us to take a more complete look at this type of conversation. How dialogue is defined is crucial to its incorporation in postformal conversation.

Donald Schön and Observational Dialogue

One form of dialogue, proposed by Donald Schön (1987), has been received in education as being a professional development possibility in the context of action research performed by career teachers (Holly, 1991), as well as being a teacher development tool that facilitates the access of student teachers to the professional community (Mackinnon & Grunau, 1994). However, some educators have criticized Schön's work on the grounds that his reflection is based on observation (Louden, 1992). Louden interprets Schön's reflection as "reports of action generated by observers rather than by participants," which may be appropriate for "design, management, engineering, planning, counseling, music" but not for education

(p. 178). Louden's point is two-fold: that educational research provides opportunities to move beyond observation toward participation in the action; and that well-developed collaborative relationships are necessary for participative research.

Jürgen Habermas and Critical Dialogue

Where Schön's and Louden's reflective tools tend to focus on the development of methodology (the curriculum and the instructional aspects of an educational system), Jürgen Habermas (1995) and other critical social theorists have come to speak of critical social science as a way of organizing collaborative critical research by groups committed to shared struggle against unjust and irrational forms of social life. Critical social science is a participatory form of social research which aims at identifying and stating the ideological character of social life as a problem, and at overcoming these constraints through shared reflection and action (Kemmis, 1987).

Habermas's version of dialogue (1995) is a synthesis of pragmatism and hermeneutics in which epistemic authority is located in the community and validated through collaborative communication, culminating in a common understanding that is unconditional. This critical dialogue leads not only to better practice but also to change in how we organize ourselves (systemic structures) and in how we act with and to each other (systemic relationships). Habermas's critically contextualized dialogue is more in tune than other dialogues with the requirements of a post-formal conversation.

David Bohm and Dialogue

Another form of dialogue, which is central to post-formal conversation, was derived from David Bohm's examination of thought as a system. This examination provides a new perspective on the problem of educational change. Bohm saw thought as a system where feeling and thought interpenetrate one another, where thought and knowledge are collective phenomena (1990, 1992).

An implication for educational change is that improvement cannot occur individually since thought is "a systemic phenomenon arising from how we interact and discourse with one another" (Senge, 1990, p. 240). The antithesis of this systemic view is the piecemeal approach in which educators deal with problems by reacting to symptoms instead of engaging the holistic nature of the problem of the failure of educational change. Educators erroneously fragment the problem into isolated bits and lose sight of the greater meaning of the problem. This was continuously evident in the ways in which the participants viewed educational change. Dave saw the problems with change initiatives as directly related to administration action. In a group conversation, Barry, Dan, Steve, and Sue all focused on the students' inability to take responsibility for their actions. Barry often cited the change in administration as a main reason for the change in school culture from the 1970s to the present. Their agreement on the expulsion of dissident students as an effective means to protect the integrity of the classroom offered another example of their focus on the symptomatic aspects of the greater problem. This lack of a systemic view among the participants is a clear example of people engaging the symptoms instead of the more complex whole of the situation.

This reductionist tendency compartmentalizes schools, isolates teachers, and creates "false divisions" and "false unification" (Bohm, 1992). The participants' perceptions of themselves as separate from other stakeholders (that is, administration, students, other curricular departments, and other teachers in terms of years of experience) contributed to their isolation.

Bohm (1992) speculated that thought is participatory, as compared to the notion that thought is neutral knowledge that we decide to use. To a participant, thought is an active agent shaping how people interact with others (Senge, 1990). In a symbolic interactionist context, the views of the participants in this study toward other stakeholders in their school (that is, students, administrators, and younger teachers) were reciprocated. For example, if a student resisted the management procedures and pedagogy of one of the participants, the student's action would reinforce the original thoughts held by the participant about the student. This mutually reinforcing interaction of thoughts and attitudes further contributes to the balkanized and individualized school culture.

Other implications of the participatory nature of thought are that the real power in change initiatives is in the activity of thought, and that, in their thinking, teachers are products of the collective culture. If change is proposed and the method of reform creates confusion and polarization in the thinking of the teachers, the initiative will fail. The demise of the open-space initiative resulted from confusion in vision and in motivation. The resultant polarization was manifested in the balkanization of the faculty. However, if the teachers as a group can discern significant meaning in the change or generate their own change initiative, the chances of successful change increase. The teacher empowerment and teacher ownership in the initial development of the open-space initiative reveals this.

But whatever the scenario, control over the outcome lies in what and how the teachers think. Thought processes that result in confusion are counterproductive to the successful implementation of change. Bohm identified this confusion as incoherence of thought.

Incoherence is characterized as inconsistency, conflict, contradiction, and stress (Bohm, 1992). "You want to do something but it doesn't come out as you intend" (Bohm, 1992, p. 10). Teachers who are unaware of the hidden consequences of their practice are experiencing incoherence. For example, teachers, who are egalitarian by nature, may be unaware that their use of traditional grading practices results in sorting, ranking, and promotion of competition, in turn reinforcing classism, sexism, and racism. Incoherence is indicative of "deeper, hidden intentions," which perpetuate the problem (Bohm, 1992, p. 12). Dialectic and discussion forms of conversation prompt defensive incoherence, which is an unconscious resistance preventing us from performing the change behavior (Bohm, 1992). Conversely, coherence "is sensed as harmony, order, beauty, goodness, truth, and all that everybody wants" (p. 60).

Incoherent thinking, as seen in conversation, is problematic in many ways. Besides a general unawareness of how individual and group thoughts are affecting the change, there is the condition of systemic fault (Bohm, 1992). The fault that enervates the change effort is not isolated in one part of the system but is pervasive throughout the entire system. If implementing portfolio assessment fails to significantly improve the education of the students, is the fault with the teachers in their implementation, with the administrators who designed the portfolio in-service program, with the type of school culture, with the type of conversation, or with the vision or lack of vision in the school system? When the open-space initiative collapsed, was it because of a change in administration or because of the inability of the faculty to professionally pursue and develop the original vision? If it is a systemic fault, then it pervades all of the school system's structures and stakeholders.

Thought as Reflexive Responses

Bohm (1992) hypothesized that there are mechanisms in our thought process that operate like reflexes. These reflexive responses are conditioned through repetition and affect the emotional, physical, and intellectual aspects of teachers. When faced with change in a threatening context, these defensive reflexes engage a teacher's emotions and intellect in defense of their prior conditioning. The result is to diminish the teacher's consciousness or awareness of the real nature of the problem. When teachers "know" or "sense" that certain students are not learning and a change of method is needed, these reflexive thoughts can suppress the insight. For instance, if a teacher intuitively concludes that portfolio assessment would be an equitable and effective evaluation of student progress, this conclusion may be suppressed by the need to show that the teacher is "doing her or his job" by mathematically calculating a letter grade that is familiar to the parent, even though its primary purpose is to rank and sort the child and, by nature, is an artificial representation of the child's performance.

This conditioning of the reflexes promotes the continuation of behaviors when they are no longer appropriate. The accumulated reflexes create a "fog" that further complicates the clear perception of a situation (Bohm, 1992). An extension of the idea of reflexive thought is the idea of necessity. Bohm theorizes that some thoughts are significantly more powerful than others because besides emotion and repetition they are deemed necessary in the sense that "it cannot be otherwise" (Bohm, 1992). These thoughts are the most damaging to change initiatives and are the most frequent blocks to dialogue. If a teacher feels that order in the classroom is necessary, and that portfolios may disrupt the order, intellectual arguments will carry little weight in offsetting that thought. If a teacher believes that students are in control of their own fate, then expulsion is a viable option. The accumulated reflexive thought of teachers in stressful school environments creates a conservative "fog" that complicates the clear perception of a situation with regressive, draconian, modernistic thinking.

How Dialogue Works

Is educational discourse and consequently educational change incoherent? Is that the problem? In the context of David Bohm's theory, the choice is whether to move toward coherence, to defend incoherence, or to unconsciously perpetuate incoherence. If the decision is to move toward coherence, dialogue is the process that will reveal the incoherence. To create coherent perceptions of problems and solutions, people must learn to engage in individual and collective actions. They must describe what is happening in their thinking, see the source of their thinking, engage in self-perception, and initiate dialogue without consideration of specific questions. Coherence requires a constant testing of yourself for incoherence by inquiring whether you are getting the results that you do not want (Bohm, 1992). For incoherence to operate, it must remain hidden from the person. Dialogue will uncover our incoherent intentions.

A discussion of how Bohm's dialogue works requires a few initial thoughts. First, how people think is reflected in their conversation. If people are defensive about implementing a change, such as the introduction of portfolios, they will engage in dialectics or discussion, not dialogue. Second, thoughts are collective in nature due to the shared meaning that exists through culture. In dialogue, relationships are the most important considerations. When dialogue is working, a "oneness" arises between people, and the developing shared culture is held together by the system of thought created by its members (Bohm, 1992).

Dialogue is best conducted with the total group, not with committees of four or five. This is necessary because shared meaning is the cement that holds society together (Bohm, 1992). Schools include different subcultures (ethnic, religious, economic, age-related, and educational) that can create divisions among the members. Different views and opinions are represented; these can lead to irritation and anger, causing the whole change initiative to degenerate into yet another ineffective effort (Bohm, 1992). Generally, when change is attempted there is little large-group dialogue. Instead, most of the research, conversation, and decision making occurs in small committees. Large-group discussions of 30 to 50 people appear to be unproductive, uncontrollable, and potentially chaotic. Bohm suggests that if properly done, large-group dialogue is essential to the sharing of meanings that leads to the establishment of common purpose. When the members of a committee make the decision to change the school schedule to an intensified block schedule, they have assured the necessity of dialectics and discussion to get the rest to "buy in" to the decision. The commitment to sustained dialogue involving the whole group is a radical and frightening idea for most schools However, without it, education will continue to be divided in purpose and ineffective in meeting the needs of an information society.

In this study the participants recognized the need to include other stakeholders (that is, administrators and younger teachers) in a conversation but had no confidence that a more inclusive conversation could be effective. The inclusion of students was not viewed as an option. Interestingly the participants also felt that an effective implementation of dialogic conversation could only occur in small groups. Their lack of confidence in large groups was evident in the in-service proposal to the administration which asked for small groups of teachers instead of a conversation including all the faculty. Also in the proposal, topics such as teaching in the block schedule and classroom management were suggested as focal points instead of more generative questions dealing with systemic vision and organizational purpose.

Large-group dialogue can be properly carried out if dialogue itself is the purpose. "Dialogue does not preceed from imposing a purpose or an intention" (Bohm, 1992, p. 193). The members of faculty would start by talking about dialogue (which is actually talking about community), not about a current initiative or problem. Meaning and significance may occur after dialogue sustained over weeks, not during the course of one faculty meeting. Purposes will change, but the group must stay focused on the development of meaning that will occur through the deconstruction of the participants' "individual conditioning" and through the deconstruction of the school culture. Not everyone will agree, but all must listen to every thought and see its meaning (Bohm, 1992). "From the meaning flows the sense of value, and from that flows the purpose and the action" that can result in meaningful change (Bohm, 1992, p. 207). "Something with great significance will generate a sense of value. And the value is the energy that infuses you; it makes you feel it's worth doing, or worthwhile" (Bohm, 1992, p. 194). After a while the participants will agree on what is necessary, valuable, and worthwhile.

Bohm (1992) describes dialogue as the following process. No advance agenda should be used. Instead, the group should explore thought free of authority. Initially, incoherence and defensive reflexes will emerge. Then people will see the extent of the defenses and the ways in which the images that they hold in place are protected. There will be a constant need to deconstruct beliefs in relation to what causes and maintains them. Problems will be encountered. Some people will need to dominate; others will be reticent. Resentment and role-playing, along with the different basic assumptions in the group, will lead to reflexive emotional behavior that may, in turn, create polarization. People may resist each other instead of working together; emotions will spread throughout the group. The assumptions that people make are embedded in the culture. To change these assumptions, the knowledge and processes of the culture need to be changed. This can only be accomplished by eliciting these assumptions and allowing them to be challenged. To change the culture, all members of the culture must participate. "Doing it together means that we're communicating, facing all these issues and whatever happens persisting and sustaining the work even when it becomes difficult and unpleasant" (Bohm, 1992, p. 226). This persistent collective dialogue taps into the flow of meaning from which we can gain direct insight into the collective movement of thought and benefit from the collective intelligence (Bohm, 1992).

Engaging in Dialogue

Teacher Talk suggests that the type of dialogue theorized by Bohm, as opposed to Schön but including the criticality of Habermas, is the type of dialogue necessary to drive a post-formal inquiry by a school. This is the type of dialogue that an administrator who emulates Sergiovanni's model would encourage, along with the "followership" techniques of motivation. How then would a faculty engage in dialogue?

Hypothetically, if a faculty engaged in dialogue it could possibly proceed in this manner. At an early faculty meeting, the principal would briefly explain the following. A series of meetings, spread throughout the year, will be dedicated to group dialogue. There will be no prearranged agenda because the purpose of the conversation will be to explore what and how we think about education. Hopefully, the outcome will be the development of common thoughts and meanings about education at our school. If nothing practical comes from this dialogue, perhaps we will learn more about each other and about education at our school.

A brief presentation by a facilitator would follow. This presentation would highlight the essential theory of the forms of conversation and introduce the idea that during the conversation teachers should think on two levels. They should engage the issue at hand but also be aware of the dynamics of the conversation. Teachers would be told that more detailed information is available in the professional library for their perusal.

At this time the conversation would begin. More than likely, initial conversation would be tentative and issue oriented, rather than philosophical or theoretical. Issues deemed immediately relevant would dominate the conversation. Issues such as faculty parking, inequities in extracurricular duty assignments, and budget cuts would be considered mundane by an outsider but germane and vital to the faculty. As the year progressed, issues might become more global, theoretical, and philosophical. However, this would depend on faculty perceptions of administrative commitment, administrative intent, and power. The nature of the issues would be of secondary importance because, regardless of the issues involved, personalities, emotions, relationships, and individual and collective thoughts would surface. The effects of the balkanization, individualization, and contrivance of the culture (Hargreaves, 1994) would be evident. The initial conversation would be typical of dialectical and discussion forms.

Prior to the end of the first meeting, the facilitator would ask the faculty to consider questions about what happened during the conversation.

These questions would be reflective and explore areas such as the identification of the issues, who supported them and why, the emergence of emotion and how people felt about it; the possible polarization of faculty thinking; and issues of control, power, and domination. Finally the facilitator might ask the teachers to describe the culture of the school. After time for reflection, the second meeting could open with a discussion of these questions, as well as with another brief instructional dialogue about conversation.

As the year progressed, this pattern of conversation, reflection, and instruction could continue or be supplanted by a routine determined by the group. This forum could provide a springboard for the development of additional related skills such as listening, problem solving, critical thinking, or any others identified by the group as essential. As the faculty's skills developed, this process of professional development could be applied to student development in the teachers' classes. Faculty use of these skills and processes in their classes would be the proof of significant professional growth.

An example of how this conversation could involve the change process would be the inclusion of an anticipated change such as the change to an intensive block schedule. This type of issue would include all of the dynamics described by Bohm. Positions would be staked out, dialectics used, and strong emotions evident in discussion. Critical reflection on this discussion would unmask the hidden reflexes and provide an opportunity for the group members to learn about how they currently change and how they could do it better. Encouraging people to think about a volatile issue on two levels might create a more dialoguelike environment, providing opportunities for coherent thought that could lead to insight as well as to collegial culture.

All of us who participated in the research feel that this scenario faces obvious problems in the real world. Besides pointing out the very real lack of time for professional development and planning, a modernist would group this activity together with values clarification and other denounced "touchy-feely" ideas. Real commitment on the part of the holders of power (in most cases the administration) would be critical because of the issues of power and control that would inevitably be raised. Contexts of race, gender, and class would emerge as the reflection evolved to critical levels. The question of outcomes would be problematic. Participants would ask where is this going, what will we gain, and how will we assess the effort? The indeterminacy and unpredictability of the direction of this venture would create insecurities that would threaten commitment. Specifically, people entrenched in modernistic paradigms would find it hard to understand postmodern meaning in a postmodern process.

Participant Thoughts on Dialogue

Despite this pessimistic outlook, people always return to the idea of dialogue as a potentially positive experience. After participating in a series of meetings with the superintendent concerning some issues raised by the teachers' union, Barry revised his negative opinion of the administration:

Barry: I think that one of the major things that occurred [in these meetings] was a realization on my part that the superintendent is really a person who is interested in education. As I think about this situation I am beginning to think that maybe there is a tinge of hope, because I think that if we continued to meet with him to exchange ideas, we could achieve a degree of collegiality. Maybe the problem is with the people between the superintendent and us. Maybe they are incapable of being collegial.

Ray: What type of conversation did you expect to have with the superintendent?

Barry: Dialectic and discussion. What I got was dialogue. I really felt that he sincerely wanted to come to a common agreement that would be best for the school.

Ray: How did that make you feel personally as a professional?

Barry: I thought that I was treated with respect and collegiality. I thought that I was an equal as far as the decisions that were being made.

Ray: How would you try to promote this type of conversation elsewhere in the school culture?

Barry: I think one of the ideal ways to begin would be through small volunteer group meetings. I'm going to say with the principals because that is the level where it has to begin. But I don't believe the principal or the assistant principal is equipped to deal with situations like this on the same level as the superintendent. I believe that the superintendent has a self-assurance and self-confidence that doesn't exist on the high school administrative level. They are insecure, and I don't think that they have the ability to operate on that level of conversation.

The collegial meetings with the superintendent created a disequilibrium in Barry's interpretation of the possibility of the administration and the faculty working together in a nonadversarial manner to solve educational problems. However, his reflexive response maintained the reductionist incoherence of his thinking by separating the administration into two groups (the superintendent and the principals). This allowed him to accommodate the change in his thinking about administrative behavior and motivation (the superintendent) and still maintain his old beliefs about the adversarial nature of the principals. Instead of focusing on the development of dialogue and the dialogical process, Barry is still focusing on the narrow reductionist explanation of why things are the way they are.

At one point in an individual interview, Sue intuitively agreed with Bohm's idea of the whole group engaging in open conversation. However, she immediately qualified the openness aspect:

Sue: When does this kind of dialogue ever occur? It doesn't. There is no avenue for this kind of dialogue to occur. There is nothing built in to the "system" that will ask for this kind of dialogue. Individuals can talk with individuals, but we never have these open dialogues as groups. I do think that administrators tend to be gun shy about these, and rightfully so because you end up having a huge gripe session. I think that they perceive group dialogue as a huge gripe session that tends to be unproductive. Although I don't know because we never have them.
Ray: Would conversations like this be a valuable activity?
Sue: The in-service days should be exactly what we are talking about. Where there isn't anything planned. Where you have open dialogue about issues that concern people. People could throw out issues that concern them, and maybe there are people who through this open dialogue would have solutions. A time when people could present problems or concerns, and their colleagues, in a collegial way, could offer ways of handling them. Or, if nothing else, empathize with them. People don't always have solutions for your problems, but it is nice to know that there is someone who cares about your concerns. However, I do think that these conversations have to be guided a little bit, because you can get into a situation where it becomes a massive gripe session; and how do you avoid that?

Sue's concern about dialogic conversation disintegrating into a "gripe session" is a real concern for two reasons. First, a gripe session would be construed by any administrator as a threatening, unproductive situation. Because of this, Sue correctly assumed that most administrators (at least the ones in her school) would assiduously avoid this type of situation. Therefore, guarantees would have to be made by the faculty that a gripe session would not develop. Guarantees of this kind were included in the in-service proposal given to the administration for time to be set aside for dialogic conversation. However, a second concern is the importance of a gripe session in the development of community through the dialogic process. The issues brought out during a gripe session would be fundamental issues dealing with power. The griping would be a manifestation of the frustration of the teachers and the apparent (as interpreted by the teachers) misuse of power on the part of the administrators. The griping would be an act of resistance by the teachers to their lack of ownership in policy making. The griping and the subsequent dialectical conversation would be a necessary part of the dialogic process. Teacher assumptions must be evoked, otherwise these assumptions and the related assumptions of the administration cannot be challenged. The challenging of all assumptions is a central aspect of post-formal thinking.

The Safety of Roundtables

Roundtables can be used to reduce the anxiety created by the specter of conversation turning into a gripe session. A roundtable is a conversational form that would provide a "safer" environment in which stakeholder frustrations could be vented and opposing positions heard by all participating stakeholders. Roundtables take various forms; however, the following two formats would serve the dual purpose of allowing stakeholders to voice their opinions, and to providing conversational control that would accommodate all possible stakeholder anxieties.

The first form places the participating stakeholders in a circle. Each participant receives a time-credit (in the form of a piece of paper; however, stones, sticks, or other items can be used) that allows a person to speak once. If participants wish to speak, they give the time-credit to the facilitator and then speak uninterrupted, either for a predetermined amount of time or for as long as they care to speak. Other options are not using the time-credit (not speaking) or giving it to another person (giving away your voice). The role of the facilitator is simply to ask who wishes to speak, to recognize speakers, and to collect the time-credits. The roundtable ends when no one wishes to speak or all time-credits are expended. The only rule is that no one may deny another's voice by talking, whispering, laughing, or engaging in any other behaviors that interfere with a person who is speaking. To engage in such behaviors is to deny someone's voice. Of course, variations can be made in this format to accommodate the uniqueness of the situation or the time available.

The other roundtable structure is different in that five chairs are placed inside the circle. Participants can volunteer to sit in these chairs, or a prior arrangement can be made to ensure that all stakeholder factions are represented in the middle. Those in the middle are the speakers; all those in the outside circle are listeners. Once again, all participants receive one time-credit. This roundtable starts with each of the participants seated inside the circle making a speech proposing a position or expressing an opinion about anything that the speaker wishes to talk about. Of course, a prior topic could be selected to direct the conversation. At the conclusion of the five speeches, those in the outer ring give their time-credits to the speaker whose position they want to hear more about. All participants have the option to not pass their voice to another. The person who receives the most time-credits speaks first, and thereafter each of the speakers are able to speak until their time-credits are depleted. Those in the center have a voice; those in the outer ring can only give their voice to others.

Heiner Benking (1997) describes numerous variations on this technique. Roundtables can be used to guarantee voices for all factions in a school in a controlled manner. The safety provided by roundtables facilitates the necessary dialectical and emotional conversation that is the first step in moving toward community.

Post-Formal Thinking as Conversation

Post-formal conversation embodies dialogue and design conversation and provides a mechanism to transcend reflexive thought. Therefore it is central to postmodern professional development and consequently to the change that is relevant to postmodern problems. William Doll's characterization of the postmodern curriculum as "rich, recursive, relational, and rigorous" (1993, p. 176) is an apt description of conversation performed in the context of post-formal thinking. Post-formal conversation can be characterized as collective post-formal thinking. Just as Kincheloe (1993) sees post-formal thinking about thinking as "a running meta-dialogue, a constant conversation with self" (p. 146), so post-formal conversation would be a constant conversation among educators about the etymology, patterns, process, and contextualization of educational issues and experiences. As post-formal thinking is an "expansion of self-awareness and consciousness" (Kincheloe, 1993, p. 146), post-formal conversation includes an expansion of the awareness of self in relation to others and a critical awareness of the communication process in relation to the ways in which it emancipates or constrains our relations with others. The techniques of post-formal conversation can be used to deal with the systemic fault wrought by the incoherence and reflexive response of modernistic thought.

Seldom do educational practitioners engage in reflective thinking that entails a consideration of the origins of their culture, the way their knowledge is produced (etymology), the deeper, more complex systemic realities of their situation (patterns), the apparent certainties of their professional lives (process), and the intricate context of their setting (contextualization). When educational change or an educational problem occurs, how often does the community that must engage the problem pause and converse about the relationship of their culture to the problem, the ways in which the problem is embedded or will affect the subsystems in the school system, the need to rethink what they believe to be certain, or the importance of place and time to the change or problem? Unfortunately, this holistic, more complete procedure is often viewed as superfluous or unproductive.

Post-formal thinking critiques and extends the Piagetian formalism of cognition by including critical considerations of power as contextualized by issues such as race, gender, class, sexual preference, age, and ethnicity. Additionally, post-formal thinking (and interaction in post-formal conversation) expands our awareness of the origins of knowledge, the deep hidden patterns that shape our construction of reality, and the need to deconstruct the texts that limit our potential (Kincheloe & Steinberg, 1996). Post-formal conversation is a dynamic investigation of our selves, our relations with others, and the political implications of the type of conversation in which we are engaged. Since the political implications affect gender, class, age, race, and ethnicity, post-formal conversation includes a crucial ethical component.

The political implications of conversation and the accompanying moral component must be framed by a consideration of power. Therefore, post-formal conversation is a dialogue about power. All conversation has a political or power component, and post-formal conversation in education is about teachers becoming aware of and eventually exercising power. Teacher recognition and use of power is not limited to curriculum and instruction, it extends to all systemic components of the community and those that affect the community. Empowered teachers must post-formally critique all the actions of other societal interests that attempt to influence education. This critique would include seemingly diverse actions such as state mandates, media representations of American education, and the appropriation of youth culture for commercial gain.

Post-formal strategies that would facilitate a teacher's professional development include critical reflection on past, present, and future experience. This temporal strategy would be like William Pinar's process of "currere" (Pinar, 1994). Also, a social psychoanalysis of place (Kincheloe & Pinar, eds. 1991) would unveil the historical antecedents of the teacher's current reality and aid in the reconstruction of the teacher's essential meanings as they are affected by the teacher's setting.

Educators must be aware that "if meanings are in people and if the people change, then meanings change" (Faules & Alexander, 1978, p. 8). The potential for change is located in people and in their constructions of reality. When people are attempting to change, the type of conversations becomes critical. Dialectic and discussion conversation solidify and reinforce entrenched meanings about objects, people, and situations. The adversarial nature of these types of conversation validates the differences in meanings between two groups. Positions are polarized, and the purpose of conversation is to win. On the other hand, dialogue in the context of post-formal thinking redefines conversation as a collective attempt to accommodate the divergent meanings to create workable spaces for the inclusion of difference as a benefit to the system.

Making Sense of Post-Formal Conversation

A different way of looking at conversation is to see all conversation as either generative or strategic (Avers et al. 1996; Banathy, 1996a; Bohm, 1990). Banathy distinguishes between generative and strategic dialogue by describing the purpose of the former as the generation of "a common frame of thinking, shared meaning, and a collective world view in a group" (1996a, p. 39). Strategic dialogue "implies communication among designers [of educational sytems] that focuses on the specific task of seeking solutions" (Banathy, 1996a, p. 39). Whereas strategic dialogue intends to achieve specific outcomes or products through a focused and time-driven process, generative dialogue is not product oriented but is open ended and cannot be time-bound (Avers et al., 1996). "Generative dialogue is conversation of the heart whereas strategic dialogue is conversation of the mind" (Avers et al., 1996, p. 13). Generative dialogue recognizes the necessary inclusion of emotion in any attempt to create meaning. All change creates uncertainty and anxiety that represent real, vital concerns. Generative dialogue lays the foundation for the moral commitment that drives substantive change.

Design conversation is a compilation of generative dialogue and strategic dialogue in a dynamic interactive relationship (Banathy, 1996a). Even though each phase is "a fundamentally different and interdependent process" (Avers et al., 1996, p. 13), both phases are necessary in the design process and affect not only the outcome of the change but also each other. In a culture that values "quick fixes," change is often doomed when those involved rush to "strategic dialogue without first engaging in the formative work of the generative phase" (Avers et al., 1996, p. 14). Also, failure in the strategic dialogue phase will negate the effectiveness of the vision making of stakeholders who share beliefs, values, and goals.

Therefore, the proposition is that design conversation, with its generative and strategic aspects, is an integral part of post-formal conversation.

Design conversation brings a number of aspects to the mix: safety, trust, vision, consensus in some form, the recognition of emotion, transcendence, and the idea of inclusion through collaboration. The generative dialogue of design conversation allows individuals to transcend their backgrounds and limitations (Avers et al., 1996). It allows them to empty themselves of mindsets that interfere with the realization of the vision. André Dolbec recognizes the collaborative nature of change by applying a gestalt approach to the design process, which "helps to create an environment where individual and group concerns can be properly integrated and harmonized" (1996, p. 17). This integration could be a result of an ideal consensus where everyone is like-minded, or, if the situation is oppositional, consensus could be in the form explicated by Elizabeth Ellsworth: "If you can talk to me in ways that show you understand that your knowledge of me, the world, and 'the Right thing to do' will always be partial, interested, and potentially oppressive to others, and if I can do the same, then we can work together on shaping and reshaping alliances for constructing circumstances in which students of difference can thrive" (1989, p. 324).

Post-formal thinking is inherently compatible with design conversation in its generative methods of reflection and metaphor. The critical reflection and the psychoanalytical curiosity about linguistic labels or symbols deals with matters of the heart as well as with the suspension of previous mindsets. Arne Collen (1996) identifies a key concept of design inquiry that also applies to post-formal thinking: confluence, not mergence or expansion, is the key outcome.

Post-formal thinking contributes a holistic concept of cognition that frames the integration of intellect and emotion in the critical context of power. As design conversation recognizes the collaborative nature of change, post-formal thinking adds difference or diversity to the conversation. Indeed, change involves people collaborating either collegially or in a contrived manner. However, effective change requires an awareness of how diversity and difference affect that collaboration. Also, processes such as "currere" as well as considerations of place contribute to the requisite condition of transcendence. Finally, moral commitment is achieved as individuals and groups approximate what Paolo Freire calls conscientization or critical consciousness (Freire & Macedo, 1996). Post-formal thinking encourages the ability of people to analyze and problematize the sociopolitical, economic, and cultural realities that shape their lives (Freire & Macedo, 1996). This critical consciousness leads to the inclusion of such realities in the design conversation. The critical nature of post-formal thinking puts a harder edge on the actions that result from post-formal conversation. The grindstone of resistance to inequitable displays of power hones this edge.

Thus, design conversation and post-formal thinking constitute post-formal conversation. A return to two previous situations will confirm this conclusion. Applying the lens of post-formal conversation to the situation of Mrs. B, reveals a person who had minimal involvement in the generative dialogue. In situations like hers, people other than the teacher (administrators, school boards, experts) make key decisions: Is there a problem with instruction? What changes should be made? What type of training is necessary to achieve the goals? What will be the systemic effects of the change? In my experience, when teachers are allowed to participate in change, their inclusion is often limited to the strategic conversation phase, and it is further constrained by a dialectical conversation controlled by those in power (obviously not the teachers).

In the social studies situation detailed in Chapter One, to a degree design conversation initially occurred when the social studies teachers were engaged in creating something new; however, the conversation was dominated by certain members of that department. When other members raised concerns, they were excluded from any generative or strategic dialogue. Through the years, as the social studies department became balkanized, its members' conversation became solely strategic, finally resulting in only one faction participating in the dialogue. All other conversation was of a dialectical, defensive nature. As the years passed, the conversation was no longer dialogic due to the loss of certain dialogical characteristics such as suspension of mindsets, recursiveness, critical reflection, acceptance of emotion, and inclusion of other stakeholders. Important considerations in post-formal conversation are trust, safety, and respect. These are key achievements of the dialogic process, because they represent the accommodation of that which causes fear and anxiety. The denial of emotion and the exclusion of stakeholders because of a failure to critically reflect and suspend mindsets disallow the development of trust, safety, and respect. Obviously, these key elements were not among the characteristics of change in this department or this school.

My research is based upon the recognition of the primacy of conversation in professional development as it relates to the topic of change. This recognition includes the necessity of being aware of all forms of conversation and the development of conversational skills related to post-formal conversation. A post-formal reconceptualization of professional development recognizes the following phases in relevant and effective professional development—a generative phase followed by a strategic phase characterized by equitable stakeholder ownership in all phases. The development of an environment conducive to a generative process is a precondition that must be met. The attainment of requisite skills and knowledge will be an on-going process throughout any professional development phase, not just a prerequisite for post-formal professional development.

In conclusion, I reiterate that post-formal conversation is a necessary component of any change attempt that specifically targets the problems resulting from the intersection of the postmodern condition and modernistic interventions. Post-formal conversation is a synergetic compilation of dialogic conversation as explicated by Bohm, design conversation, post-formal thinking, and generative conversation. The synergy of post-formal conversation will be heightened by the inclusion of affect theory, the formation of egalitarian communities, and systems thinking.

Affect Control Theory

Returning to the narrative in Chapter One, as the social studies faculty became increasingly alienated from the other members of their school community, the social studies teachers became more objective, technical, and standardized. Student, teacher, parent, and administrative dissent from and criticism of the social studies program was frequently viewed by the social studies teachers as hysterical and emotional. This interpretation which emphasized the objective and denied the emotional, further exacerbated the social studies department's estrangement from the rest. Basically, the social studies department concluded that its objective and rational demeanor was a more valid way of uncovering the "truth" of the situation than the emotional reactions of those who opposed the program. The rational and objective social studies department was right, and the emotional others were wrong.

A situation like this is typical in that emotion is often excluded from the educational mix. American schools have relegated emotion to the playing field and extracurricular activities. When students enter the classroom they must get serious, stop being silly, and get on task. When students are placed in longer instructional blocks, current restructuring efforts play lip service to emotion by recognizing the deleterious nature of boredom. However, modernistically oriented educators invariably maintain the archaic separation of the intellect and emotion through the continuation of dry, unnatural pedagogical strategies of worksheets, lectures, movies, and rigidly controlled group work. Affect never left the classroom; it was merely repressed. Recognition of student and teacher emotion is usually relegated to classroom management and teacher control contexts. But for educational change to be successful on any level, affect must be recognized and nurtured in all educational contexts.

As affective associations are provoked by words, so the language and symbolization of schooling is designed to evoke affective responses. This symbolization acts as part of the controlling mechanisms of centralized, authoritarian schools. The self-esteem of teachers is fair game in administrative attempts to maintain control. In traditional schools, faculty meetings reveal of the manipulation of teacher affect through seating arrangements (administrators in positions denoting authority), control of the agenda (produced by the administrator), control of time and attendance (mandatory meetings of a specific length, with absenteeism requiring administrative approval), and feeling tone (upbeat if the administration determines that teachers are doing their jobs, chastising if they are not). The intent of these manipulations is to control teachers by eliciting feelings of subordination. In many schools the issue of teacher dress, especially the requirement that male teachers wear ties and dress shirts, is a conscious attempt to communicate messages of professional superiority (administrators in suits) and inferiority (teachers in shirts and ties).

A typical faculty meeting that took place in the participants' school during the course of this research involved the principals standing in front of the faculty members, who were seated in rows in a lecture hall. The agenda of the meeting was given to the faculty members after they were seated. At that time the principal proceeded to go through the agenda reading and explaining each item. Beyond occasional questions by teachers, which were answered by the principal, no conversation of any kind ensued. Any controversial issues (consistency in the administration's enforcement of the discipline policy, management of the Alternative Education program) were placed at the end of the agenda. This assured a minimum of available discussion time for these issues, due to the time limit imposed on the length of the meeting by the union contract. When this limit was reached, the meeting would abruptly end, truncating any discussion of the controversial issues. At one meeting that was differently organized, open discussion was allowed earlier in the meeting. The principal opened the discussion with the comment, "You may not have this chance [to engage in open discussion] again for quite a while." The main issue was faculty concern about the operation and effectiveness of the Alternative Education program. The adversarial relationship between the administration and the faculty was evident in the type of conversation that occurred and in the control of the meeting by the administrator. All faculty comments were directed at the principal, who either defended the administration's handling of the program or attacked various faculty members as not being "team players." This dialectic-and-discussion type of conversation persisted through the whole meeting. As the principal engaged one teacher at a time, the rest of the faculty were engaged in grumbling, whispering, and making assorted side-comments. The principal's position that the failings of the program should be attributed to the teachers' lack of support later surfaced in the minutes of the Meet and Discuss Committee meeting, which comprises representatives of the teachers' union and the administration. After a period of confrontation punctuated by a mixture of anxiety, frustration, and hostility, the faculty meeting ended with nothing resolved. Once again the administration maintained control of the decision-making process, and the faculty appeared to be in emotional disarray.

As mentioned, the self-esteem of teachers is considered fair game in using affect to control them. One of the most insidious side effects of the isolation of teachers is the effect on their affect. For instance, throughout the interviews Dave was consistently hostile toward the administration in particular and the school system in general. He would become visibly disturbed when reflecting on his experiences. In a similar vein, Barry's frustration and hostility would become apparent when talking about the "old days of the 1970s" versus his experience with his peers and the administrators during the 1980s and 1990s. Affectively, all the participants would exhibit agitation and then resignation when retelling and interpreting their experience. It became apparent that their current professional attitudes and actions were a result of the interrelationship between their culture, their affective associations, and their type of daily conversation. The attitudes and actions of these teachers were those of people who essentially work in isolation from other professionals, who constantly engage in dialectical and discussion conversation, and who have strong negative feelings about their situation, other stakeholders, and, in some cases, themselves.

Most notably affected from a self-esteem perspective was Sue. Toward the end of the first interview, I asked her how she felt about the kind of conversation that we were having. Up to this point in the interview, her conversation contained numerous self-deprecating comments. Typically after a particularly insightful comment, she would belittle her reflection:

> Sue: It is a very different experience. I don't feel like I am put on the spot, but I feel like I sound stupid in places. These are things that you don't ever think about out loud, and I think that I'm sounding incoherent sometimes. And there are things that I just never really thought about. At least I never verbalized them. But I don't feel uncomfortable. I feel real comfortable, but I have known you for a long time, and I know that this isn't

being used to make me sound like I am an idiot. I am doing quite an adequate job of that myself.

Ray: Not at all.

Sue: I feel like I am not answering. I feel like I am not at all answering what you are asking me.

Ray: Do you think the things that you are bringing up are valuable?

Sue: Yes.

Ray: Things that may benefit you in some way?

Sue: Yes, because I do have to take a look. You know there comes a time when you are talking about something that has been your career that you have got to take a look at. I mean it is something that you have spent your entire life doing.

At this time Sue began to cry and said, "I don't know why I am doing this." She composed herself and continued:

You know the last few years I don't feel like I am a good teacher any more; but I put so much time into it. I don't know why I feel that way. You think that you will get to the end of your career, and you realize you weren't good at what you spent your whole life doing, and you don't have another round to go. This is it.

Ray: Do you feel professionally isolated?

Sue: Very much so, but I think that I bring that on myself. I have become isolated, and that might be part of my problem. I have completely withdrawn from everyone. I don't leave my room except to go to the bathroom or to the office. I have virtually no contact with anyone, and I have been this way for the last five or six years. I don't know why that is. I don't know why I have done this, but I don't have contact with anyone. You know I work like hell. I really work hard. I still don't think that there is anyone on the faculty who works harder than I do. I used to really think that I was good. Now I work really hard and think that I am not that good any more. There's something really wrong. I am in here on weekends, and this summer I was in here for two and a half weeks before school started, putting in eight-hour days. But I don't feel good about what I do any more. I used to, but not any more. And change, you know, I mean it is constant. You get barraged from everyone. You get barraged in the papers [news media]. The parents don't care, and it seems like the kids don't care. The administration is giving lip service to this, but I don't think they really care. I don't think anybody really cares. It's hard. I mean this isn't even what we are supposed to be.

Ray: Do you think there is any connection between the fact that you are now professionally isolated and the fact that there was no isolation in the open space?

Sue: That might have something to do with it.

Ray: Did your peers validate what you did when you interacted with them?

Sue: That might be it. Part of this does trace back to when we came into the self-contained rooms from the open classroom. Unlike a lot of people, the English department really liked the open classroom. I hadn't thought about that, but that might directly relate to my isolation. Maybe I was getting more validation. You know how you feel when things are just clicking and you are really on. For a period of three or four years, I knew I was really on. I was really in sync with the students, and I knew I was doing a good job. Then it just stopped. You know it may correspond with Carolyn leaving [Carolyn was a colleague who left the profession for health reasons], and with us moving over to this side of the building. Maybe going from the open classroom was part of it.

Ray: Just for the record, I would assume that currently you see people very little during the day except when you stand in the hall between classes?

Sue: Right.

Ray: And in the old days in the open area?

Sue: We saw people all of the time. We talked to one another all of the time, we called out to one another, and we would consult with one another about things that came up.

Her peers and administrators consider Sue a consummate professional. She constantly participates in cutting-edge programs from whole language to the most recent state writing programs. Her expertise and work ethic are unimpeachable. When the transcripts were exchanged, Barry could not believe Sue's comments about herself. To him, for Sue to see herself in this way was unfathomable. How then does such a complete professional develop such negative self-perceptions? The answer, at least for Sue, lies in the deleterious effects of isolation created by a balkanized and individualized school culture, the lack of generative feedback through post-formal conversation, and the incapacitation wrought by negative affective associations.

Affect, which is attached to the symbolic representation of social interactions, can be systemically manipulated. Therefore, affect is a vital area of exploration in post-formal conversation. The idea that socially constructed meaning is shaped by affective associations of language has implications for teacher talk and for objects of consciousness shared by teachers. As language becomes a control mechanism, so do affective associations. In the Chapter One narrative, as the relationship between the administration and the social studies department became more adversarial, the administration used the fears and frustrations of other faculty about the open school to support their goal of a return to a completely traditional curriculum. These fears and frustrations were the outcome of the other faculty members' inability to pedagogically accommodate the open-space environment and their inability to create self-contained classrooms that would accommodate their teacher-centered pedagogy. The constantly disruptive student movement and noise created a level of stress that was easily displaced onto the social studies faculty. The administration encouraged this displacement through innuendo and insinuation. A favorite tactic of the principal was to preface a critical comment about the social studies program with an unsubstantiated statement: "A number of people told me. . ." or "A number of people complained about. . ." These oppositional affective manipulations, along with the emotional state of the other faculty members facilitated a domestication of the social studies faculty in which they moved closer to the type of curriculum and instruction desired by the administration. Upon receiving the emotional support of the administration, the other faculty members quickly internalized the values and behaviors promoted by the administration.

On the other hand, the constant tension between critique and validation that was characteristic of the English department interactions in the open space created a feeling of trust that was affectively efficacious for all members of that department. Within the department there was a sense of egalitarianism because all members were individually important and all shared in the power. The social, psychological, and professional benefits of the small egalitarian community formed at that time by the English department can be realized in larger groups.

Forming an Egalitarian Community

The Ubiquitous Nature of Power

In meeting the demands of a postmodern society, educators must utilize post-formal conversation to build the moral commitment necessary for forming egalitarian communities that can better meet the needs of all members of that society. The social construction of meaning with its affective component must be viewed in a critical context of power. When viewing education systemically, it soon becomes apparent that power is an organizing feature (Sarason, 1990). Power flows throughout the system affecting culture, access to theory, validation of practice, motivation, and the professional conversation that facilitates the construction of meaning. If significant, relevant educational change is to occur, then the stakeholders (all of those participating in or affected by a system) must be empowered. Seymour Sarason (1990) sees altering power relationships as a necessary first step in reaching our educational goals. Power must be reconstituted in such a way that all stakeholders have legitimate access to policy discussions and subsequent decision making.

Empowering Teachers

Recently, education appears to be rectifying this situation by "empowering" teachers. The word is used constantly throughout professional development literature; such it is repeatedly used in the *Standards for Staff Development: High School Edition—1995*, of the National Staff Development Council and the National Association of Secondary School Principals. However, J. Dan Marshall and James T. Sears (1990) distinguish between empowerment-as-authorization, and empowerment-as-enablement. The difference is significant because the former maintains the neo-conservative conception of empowerment in which teachers and students are given limited power "to do what others prescribe," while the latter recognizes that power must be "created and realized by them—not received from or bestowed by others" (Marshall & Sears, 1990, p. 17). Marshall and Sears's discussion of empowerment is distinctive for two reasons: student empowerment is promoted, and empowerment-as-enablement is seen as a dynamic process that is "begun but never completed" (1990, p. 18).

This distinction is crucial in understanding change. Top-down mandates for changes in curriculum and instruction may result in changes that on the surface appear significantly different from traditional practice but eventually produce the same results and conditions as traditional practice. Empowering stakeholders as Sarason, Marshall, and Sears suggest results in a release of human energy and creativity that potentially can transform the schools. Recurring issues in failed reforms are teacher and student compliance and motivation. In egalitarian communities that empower teachers, these become the strengths of change initiatives that are generated and shaped by all stakeholders.

Joseph B. Shedd and Samuel B. Bacharach recognize the increasing complexity of the hierarchical structure of schools and the empowerment of teachers. While administrators are realizing that educating the "whole" student requires new systems to coordinate teacher work within a specific school or area, they also face pressures "to cut costs and eliminate repetition by centralizing and coordinating resources and activities. The traditional compromise of the administrators controlling whatever was done outside the classroom while leaving the teacher autonomous (some would say abandoned) inside the classroom will not continue to work under these pressures. The result is a hodgepodge of tacit deals among organization members, resulting in tangled hierarchies" (Shedd & Bacharach, 1991, p. xiv).

The situation in the participants' school in recent years concerning teacher empowerment is aptly described, first by Shedd and Bacharach, then by Barry through a comparison of the 1970s and the more recent situation, and finally by Dave in relation to a portfolio implementation initiative. Shedd and Bacharach report that "where employees are offered opportunities to have input into decisions made at higher levels of the organization but view such opportunities as mere formalities or attempts to create the illusion of influence, the effects of such participation are likely to be ephemeral. Indeed, such strategies often backfire and generate *more* dissatisfaction, *less* commitment, and higher levels of organizational conflict" (1991, p. 11).

In a conversation with Barry, the difference in recent years in teacher compliance and motivation concerning change initiatives and teacher empowerment became clear. I pointed out that in the recent restructuring in our high school, an extensive committee system had been established. Teachers were required to be on at least one committee that held frequent meetings, some of which lasted a very long time after the end of the school day. Many teachers became so upset with this situation that they renegotiated the part of their contract dealing with the length of the school day. The teacher reaction to this committee system was very different from the teacher reaction that accommodated the even more extensive committee system of the 1970s:

Ray: We had more committees back then than we do now. We met more often in those committees than we do now. I don't understand the difference in the teacher attitude from then to now.

Barry: The difference in attitude goes back to respect. Back in the 1970s, people volunteered for committees. People put in extra time without considering it extra time. People didn't look at the clock—check to see if their time fit the contract. The reason they didn't is because they felt involved. They felt respected. They felt that their professional rights were important. Today people won't put in any extra time, and they don't volunteer because everything comes from the top down. If anything is going to occur it has to be their [administrations'] idea, and their way. There is really no empowerment. Empowerment is merely a phrase that is used; there is no true ownership. Back in the 1970s, there was true ownership. I gave whatever time was necessary for our ideas to succeed, but today unfortunately I probably would only give what I was required to; and then I wouldn't give them all of my expertise, because of the way we are respected.

Ray: So this thing about respect and empowerment goes back to ownership?

Barry: Right.

Ray: So, of the two factors that you previously identified, ownership and the lack of a systemic view, which of those two is the most powerful to you?

Barry: Ownership. I have to feel that my opinions are respected and then valued.

Part of the recent restructuring involved the implementation of a portfolio system in the school. This program was the culmination of the work of a faculty committee. However, the decision to require all faculty to adopt the program was made by the administration. On the opening day of school, a portfolio system was presented to the faculty for immediate implementation. Eventually, due to strong faculty resistance, the program was modified, resulting in an implemented system quite different from the one on paper. Dave's comments relate to the teacher resistance to the program and the effects of this resistance on student attitudes concerning portfolios:

Ray: Who made all the decisions in the portfolio implementation?

Dave: The administration decided. It was a tease. It was like the administration said to us: Here is an idea that you guys created, and now we are going to let you run with it. And then the rug was pulled out from under the people who believed in it, and everyone became very bitter toward the program. Then the kids thought it was a joke, because it was obvious the teachers were not sold on it. Then it became a total fiasco.

Ray: So the teachers influenced student opinion on this?

Dave: I think they did in a big way because the administrators told us we had to do the program. Most teachers weren't ready for it yet, so I think that they made a joke out of it with the kids, and now every time you mention portfolios the kids get all freaked out. The kids think it is a waste of time, but it isn't—it was a great idea. However, the process didn't get off the ground because there wasn't enough time. It was another quick hit, and for me it crystallized how we try to change things. The change comes from the top with a token effort from the administration, and then when things fall apart the teachers and kids are to blame.

Student Empowerment

Those who are concerned about the involvement of students as active stakeholders in the change process will agree with Sarason's statement that "the social organization of the modal classroom is quite representative of the social organization of the school and the school system" (1990, p. 95). There is the possibility that if teachers transform their position in the system, then they will transform the position of the student in their classroom. If the teachers become transformative intellectuals as described by Giroux, their critical beliefs about themselves and their place in the system should extend to their students (Giroux, 1993). This scenario sounds like "trickle-down educationomics" (Carr, 1997), which from a systemic view would devalue students as stakeholders. However, in the real world students have no power and little chance to gain power. The only realistic chance for their empowerment is through the critical action of transformative teachers.

The teacher is the one who can engage the students in transformative activities that will encourage the development of post-formal thinking. This transformation of the student is not produced by imparting knowledge, verifying learning through assessments, or even arranging activities for the students to critically construct their own knowledge. Transformation occurs through the daily interpersonal empowerment of the student by the teacher. This can be achieved by teachers because they are in the best position to fulfill a crucial condition of critical pedagogy as espoused by Giroux—creating a safe environment for students to articulate their own positions.

The participants were cautious in discussing empowerment of students. Dan and Sue's comments neatly summarize the viewpoint of all the participants:

> Ray: What about student input? Do you think that students should have input in theoretical things as far as setting classroom policy, even in a limited way?
>
> Dan: I think in a limited way. I think where you run into danger is with something like one of our megaskills like time planning. I think that if students have too much input in setting their own deadlines, if they don't feel that they need them, then they will let deadlines go. That is a danger. I think that there have to be parameters given by the teacher.
>
> Sue: Should kids have input into curriculum? How would a kid know what should be in the curriculum? That presupposes that the kid has a knowledge base that would allow him to make decisions about what should be in the curriculum, and I'm not sure they do. There are people who are experts in certain areas. There have to be levels of expertise in society, and there have to be people who know more than other people about certain things. Hopefully, in a classroom the teacher is the one who does. Now as to whether or not kids can have input into instruction or assessment, I think that there is room for that. I don't know about curriculum because don't we have to have a certain knowledge base before we can do things, or before we can get involved in things?

These less than transformative attitudes about teacher empowerment are representative of a modernistic educational paradigm that most teachers perpetuate. Sue's comment about levels of expertise in society misses the critical point that the expert cannot provide absolute truth or direct us to the solutions for our problems. The development of egalitarian society requires the active egalitarian participation of all stakeholders.

Classroom Discipline as a Measure of Student Empowerment

The difference between transformative ideas of student empowerment and the current interaction between educators and their students can most clearly be seen in the handling of classroom discipline. The issue comes down to a choice between promoting orderliness only, or promoting a student's intellectual growth, moral maturity, and democratic potential (Butchart, 1998). Critical constructivists decry "behaviorist technologies of control and manipulation" (Butchart, 1998, p. 7), while promoting opportunities for the learner to construct social meaning in a moral context with regard for the common good and for democratic values (Butchart & McEwan, eds., 1998). The classroom opportunities promoted by critical constructivists foster skills and propensities that are essential to the development of a democratic society. These include "authentic and frequent opportunities to debate issues of principle and justice, to become comfortable with argument, disagreement and conflict, to test competing truth claims, and to engage in moral inquiry" (Butchart, 1998, p. 7).

All the teachers involved in this study care about students. However, their lack of understanding of constructivist theory, together with their paucity of experience with constructivist classroom management activities, centers them in what Michael Apple refers to as the "logic of technical control" (1986). All the classrooms of the teachers in this study are controlled, orderly learning centers. However, because of the hierarchical structure of the school and the classroom, this orderliness is "fostered through manipulation, humiliation, bribes, distance, and the primacy of technique and procedure" (Butchart, 1998, p. 10). Instead of learning appropriate behavior through "reflection and cognition," the students learn through constant observation of adults' actions to manipulate through passive resistance, implicit negotiation, classroom bargains, and group sanctions (Butchart, 1998).

The technical control these teachers effectively use is derived from their own experiences as students, techniques learned from peers, reflection upon their own trial-and-error learning within a technical control context, outside experts brought in on in-service days by the administration, and the teachers' need to survive in the classroom. Also, the teachers are quite simply products of their environment. They exist in an environment that is a replica of the one they create in their classroom. How can teachers who are essentially caring individuals risk destroying the continuously ordered state mandated by their superiors? How can they be comfortable with debate, argument, disagreement, and conflict in their classroom, when they themselves have never had professional opportunities to engage in these skills and propensities, which are indispensable to democratic interaction? The empowerment of students cannot be accomplished without the prior, and concomitant, empowerment of teachers.

What is even more telling with regard to the insidious nature of the "logic of technical control" is that an observation of my own classes would reveal the same contradictory relationship between caring for students and procedures of authoritarian control to maintain orderliness. Even though my awareness of this relationship has been broadened by my academic work, the empowerment of students and democratic interaction within my own classroom is sorely lacking. To explore this disturbing phenomenon it is necessary to take a detailed look at the systemic nature of "the logic of technical control" and the tangled hierarchies that actively resist serious attempts at stakeholder empowerment.

The Systemic View and Teachers as Systemic Agents of Change

A discussion of educational change must range from an individual perspective to a systemic perspective. Systems theory not only shows the interrelatedness of all things within a system but also the relatedness of systems to other systems. When change fails, any attempt to understand that failure must include an examination of the whole system as well as an examination of individuals. Gaining a systemic view is integral to the implementation of the new direction. The possibility of achieving the synergetic effect of the new direction is predicated upon the inclusion of an understanding of the dynamics of systems theory and systems thinking in the post-formal mix of the new direction. Specifically, achieving the synergy requires an understanding of the concepts of leverage and imperviability. Implicit in the new direction is the intent to change the system from its current modernistic form. The identification and manipulation of sites of leverage and imperviability are necessary conditions for instituting a new direction. For the purposes of this study, identifying the sites of resistance to change and the entry points that facilitate change requires an examination of systems thinking and especially of certain components of this kind of thinking, such as boundaries, progressive segregation, leading parts, and finality.

Systems Thinking

A system can be defined as "a whole that cannot be divided into independent parts. From this definition two of the system's most important properties are derived: every part of a system has properties that it loses when separated from the system, and every system has some properties—its essential ones—that none of its parts do" (Ackoff, 1981, p. 15). Systems are holistic—the study of systems is "concerned with wholes and their properties" (Checkland, 1981, p. 13). Current thinking in educational change is deficient in this holistic perspective, most often ignoring the deep structures and processes that affect the people in the system. The interrelation of power relationships, culture, conversation, moral commitment, and the construction of knowledge are some of the deep structures that are ignored by many change agents.

On the other hand, systems thinking is a way of seeing a situation as individual parts interacting to create new phenomena that can change instantaneously due to the dynamic, multifaceted processes in which the parts and the whole are engaged. A succinct definition of systems thinking is "synthesis" (Ackoff, 1981). For the participants in this study, the positive change experience of the 1970s represents such a synthesis. During this time, their increased systemic awareness allowed the creation of a new phenomenon, a community that they perceived as egalitarian. The restructuring effort of the 1990s reduced their school system to independent parts that supposedly could be manipulated and controlled. Change was restricted to curriculum, instruction, and assessment. The effect on the change of the school culture, the type of conversation, and the structure of the school was ignored, resulting in a hollow, ineffective change effort. The following applications of systems theory to educational change demonstrate how disregarding for these structures and processes creates sites of resistance to change.

Systems Imperviability and Leverage

An understanding of educational change requires a familiarity with the sites of imperviability and leverage in school systems. Imperviability implies a condition of systems incapable of being penetrated or affected by the actions of other people or by institutional structures. Leverage is the possibility of gaining a positional advantage to effect change in a system. Education's dismal track record concerning change indicates the existence of significant sites of imperviability. The key to effective change is not only to identify and work through that which is impervious to change but also to identify and develop sites of leverage that will allow the effective entry of change and change agents into a system.

Kyle Peck and Alison A. Carr (1997) express one view of leverage in educational systems. In this view, leverage is seen as variables that "emerge as better starting points than others" in "the destruction of traditional power structures" that impede change. Peck and Carr identify two attributes of variables that can be considered leverage points: they are highly modifiable and very important. Therefore, Peck and Carr theorize that if leverage points are to be found, one must look for the highly modifiable, potent variables embedded in educational systems that can be sites or opportunities for change. An examination of variables found "money" to be problematic as a leverage point due to the administration's lack of control over the school district's finances. However, vision, because it is modifiable and important, has high leverage potential, meaning that it could affect other variables in the school system. In addition, assessment of student learning has high potency as a leverage point, because it not only affects the way in which students are tested, measured, and compared to one another but it also has the *potential* to affect the teaching-learning moment (curriculum) and the perceptions of the community (public relations) (Peck & Carr, 1997).

Senge distinguishes between "high" and "low" leverage in complex situations. High leverage can provide an opportunity for "a change which, with a minimum of effort—would lead to lasting, significant improvement" (1990, p. 64). The problem is that "high-leverage changes are usually highly non-obvious to most participants in the system. They are not 'close in time and space' to obvious problem symptoms" (Senge, 1990, p. 64). Senge proposes that to attain high-leverage changes, one must learn to see the underlying structures rather than events; to think in terms of processes rather than in snapshots. This is systems thinking that "finds its greatest benefits in seeing *through* complexity to the underlying structures generating change" (1990, p. 128). To explain the non-obvious aspect of leverage and the importance of underlying structures and processes, Senge refers to the turning of an ocean-going ship. When a ship wishes to turn, a small device on the rudder called a trim tab creates a pressure differential. The turning of this device sets in motion a process that results in the turning of the ship with a minimum of energy expenditure. Understanding this process requires a apprehension of the underlying forces that are hidden from view. Likewise, in an educational system, understanding imperviability or leverage requires a comprehension of hidden mechanisms such as the interplay of power and other factors (for example, affect, conversational type, knowledge construction, and school culture).

An understanding of a system's structural levels facilitates the identification of sites of imperviability and leverage. Jenlink et al., (1996) propose that change occurs on a technology level, a people level, a structural level, or a deep value level. The technology level represents superficial change in the use of hardware, software, and other instructional material or procedures. The people level is more substantive in that roles are changed and new identities are forged. The structural level involves policy changes that have a more systemic effect. Finally, the deep value level represents changes in culture and beliefs. Resistance to change is especially strong when the change involves the people and deep value levels. These are the levels at which symbolic interaction takes place, the levels at which meaning is constructed. If significant educational change is to successfully occur, these high-leverage levels must be engaged.

The levels of change experienced by the participants involved technology and people. Dan reports on the technology changes of the 1970s:

> Dan: In the first years that I was there [the 1960s], some of the changes were just about material things. We were going to try this kind of report card instead of another kind, but there were no significant changes made in the kind of courses being taught. But then changes in academic programs started in the 1970s. There were changes in approaches to doing things within the overall program, and I felt a greater possibility for change because we were allowed to make decisions that we weren't allowed to make in earlier years.
> Dan: I think the computer has changed things within the district and has had a great effect on all levels because of the flexibility that we have in doing things. I am doing things with the computer that I would never have thought I could do without one.

Dan's comments involve the superficial changes in hardware, software, and other instructional material or procedures reported as technology-level changes. The 1970s were replete with change on this level. As reported by the participants, this period was also characterized by people-level change. Teachers became change agents and decision makers, and especially in the case of the social studies and English departments they performed some administrative functions such as scheduling students. However, there is no evidence of policy changes having a systemic effect. In fact, once in the open-space facility, most curriculum departments quickly reverted to established, traditional curriculum and instruction. Hierarchies became more rigid, power more centralized, and faculty more balkanized and individualized. At no time were deep values changed. In the late 1980s and 1990s, the restructuring effort at best fostered change on a technological level. However, even that conclusion is in doubt, due to the teacher resistance reported by the participants.

To identify sites of imperviability and leverage (primarily in the people and deep value levels) requires an examination of systemic phenomena such as conversation, praxis, culture, and power. A modernistic understanding of imperviability and leverage would seek to identify individuals, groups, techniques, and programs on the technological and structural levels as the reasons for resistance to change or as sites of potential change. However, the social construction of meaning that occurs at the people and deep value levels is the more appropriate target of those promoting substantive change. C. L. Hutchins personalizes this social construction of meaning, which should be central in a change agent's thinking and which certainly applies to the attitudes and experiences reported by the participants of this study:

> Teachers teach the way they were taught. Parents expect what they experienced in schools. Students enter schools with expectations taught to them unconsciously by the stories and remarks made by their parents. Peer pressures—among teachers and among students—reinforce these paradigms, bringing non-conforming individuals into line. These invisible expectations are at the root of why complex social systems are so difficult to change. (Hutchins, 1994, p. 23)

If educators are to construct a postmodern pedagogy, then they must be knowledgeable and adept in the use of systemic principles, in addition to the use of post-formal conversations as professional development, or they will continue to perpetuate these invisible expectations.

Systemic Boundaries

Boundaries between the subsystems within a school system are also important in understanding how school culture and structure resist change and in locating sites or individuals who potentially can leverage change. In the participants' school, systemic boundaries were different during the 1970s from the late 1980s and 1990s. In the early years, boundaries were more fluid, more permeable. People as well as ideas could more easily penetrate the individual departments (subsystems). Input and output mechanisms, which regulate the flow of information between subsystems, were more open, thus facilitating the diffusion of new ideas and the development of interdisciplinary relationships. The boundaries of the administrative and teacher subsystems allowed an interfacing that promoted collegiality and commonality of vision. As reported by the participants, the blurring of boundaries in the early 1970s allowed social relationships to develop between administration and faculty that further opened the subsystems to the diffusion of new ideas.

However, in the 1990s the balkanized culture of this school was systemically characterized by independent subsystems (departments) with rigidly guarded boundaries. Each department had closed its ranks, staked out its turf, and developed input and output regimens that would protect it from another department's incursion.

In order to promote change that would lead to more collegial interaction and possibly shared vision, a systemic view would be necessary to discern areas of leverage. One such area would be the initiation of dialogic conversation. As seen in Barry's report of his encounter with the superintendent, dialogic conversation can lead to changed perceptions and meanings about others. Dialogic conversation has the potential to transcend systemic boundaries and facilitate the construction of professional and personal relationships that can overcome imperviability.

Most reforms focus teacher attention on the technical details of their curriculum and instruction. Systemic decisions and intersystem interactions are left to the administration. Bela H. Banathy (1992) identifies and describes categories of boundaries between educational systems and other systems in the larger environment, including physical, geopolitical, economic, social, sociobiological, psychological, temporal, cultural, ethical, and technological systems. Teachers seldom deal with the input from other systems because, in traditional hierarchical and centralized systems, the boundaries are controlled by the administration. The administration makes the decisions about contact with other systems, such as Channel One (a commercial television channel), state mandates (state government system), title programs (national government system), local municipalities (local government systems), law enforcement systems, community interest groups (possibly political or religious systems), the standardized testing industry, the professional development industry, post-secondary schools, athletic clearinghouses, athletic regulatory organizations, "intermediate units," and local news media.

For instance, if a relationship is established between a public school and a vocational or technical school ("tech prep" programs), the extent of the teacher's involvement is limited to the implementation of the curricular and instructional dictates of the program. In most cases, teachers are unaware of the ramifications of this articulation on themselves and their students. Since the articulation with the other school is administratively mandated, teachers are not part of any conversation on the purposes of the program and its effects on the students. However, the systemic illiteracy also extends to the administration, which in many cases is merely following the dictates of the school board and the suprasystems (state and national mandates) in the environment. Systemic illiteracy does not permit the authentic and locally relevant construction of an educational system. Instead, the systemically illiterate educators merely react to the dictates of others. Systemic illiteracy can only be rectified by the inclusion of systemwide instruction on systems thinking and the inclusion of stakeholders in decision making.

Progressive Segregation

Ludwig Von Bertalanffy, who is generally recognized as the leader in the development of general systems theory, had a vision of systems as purposeful, self-regulating organisms striving to maintain a steady state. However, he notes that disturbances of the system can result in progressive segregation, or the splitting of the unitary system into independent causal chains that can operate independently. The result is a loss of regulability, which denigrates the whole. This "increasing determination of elements to functions only dependent on themselves" (Bertalanffy, 1968, p. 69), creates a "machine-like behavior" in which the system is now more "like a sum of independent parts" instead of a whole that is greater than its parts. An educational analogy would be a situation where the system is disturbed (state mandates are introduced), which results in the hierarchical levels and cultures (administration, individual teachers, balkanized teachers) working for independent purposes that run counter to the well-being of the whole. The failure of educational change would be akin to the "loss of regulability."

The later years (late 1980s and 1990s) as reported by the participants are characterized by progressive segregation. Currently, curricular departments vie for new staff and other resources at the expense of a smooth-running school. One department's decision to increase student enrollment in elective courses necessitates the addition of a new staff member, which precludes any increase of staff in another department. Competition of this kind between dueling departments leads to the loss of regulability, which denigrates the whole system. In this case, regulability includes collegial relationships, common vision, dialogic conversation, and systemic awareness.

Leading Parts

Another application of systems thinking is that "the more parts are specialized in a certain way, the more they are irreplaceable, and loss of parts may lead to the breakdown of the total system" (Bertalanffy, 1968, p. 70). In education the loss of an administrator or teacher may not lead to a systems breakdown. However, if this person is a "leading part," this person's departure could damage a change initiative or start a ripple affecting many different systems. This person's power may be attributed to an indefinable phenomenon such as charisma, or to a leadership style that morally empowers other stakeholders by providing spaces in which they can construct relevant, authentic change. Besides the departure of individuals who have been leading parts, the disenfranchisement or alienation of individuals or groups of stakeholders (such as teachers and students) will affect the efficacy of the whole, especially if these people are in some way indispensable to the well-being of the school.

Power is localized in these individuals and coalitions, and they can affect the actions of others in a system. In an educational context the leading part could be an administrator, a political faction on the school board, a faculty member, or a coalition of stakeholders. These leading parts can work as triggers stimulating change in the system or as resisters marshaling powerful forces against change. Individuals and coalitions outside the system in question can also function as leading parts through state mandates (OBE), textbooks (homogeneity and bias), and educational consultation.

In the 1970s the central administration, the high school principal, and the social studies and English master teachers were leading parts. As they were replaced, the shared vision crumbled and the whole system regressed to the previously traditional attitudes and procedures. Currently, the leading parts are once again administrators, whose actions perpetuate a modernistic system that continues to resist substantial change and increasingly finds it more difficult to address the needs of postmodern society.

Finality

Bertalanffy also reports a systemic characteristic called "finality." "Finality can be spoken of . . . in the sense of dependence on the future," which means that "happenings can be considered and described as being determined not by actual conditions, but also by the final state to be reached" (Bertalanffy, 1968, p. 76). This could mean that in education, change efforts are affected not only by the conditions of their implementation but also by the individual or collective interpretation of the *perceived future*. If portfolio assessment is being implemented, and teachers are following a commercially prepared formula, significant implementation progress may appear to be taking place. However, if the teachers' view is that this is a fad that will not help them in the classroom and will pass away like all fads, then the lack of stakeholder commitment will doom the long-term efficacy of this change. The teachers' interpretation of the future will affect the outcome of the change.

Finality provides a possible explanation for some of the attitudes of the participants. Their reluctance to empower students undoubtedly includes a finality component. Similarly, their lack of faith in the ability of the administration to effectively bring about substantial change, plus their lack of faith that things will get better educationally, indicate finality as a possible explanation. Any suggestion of empowering students, any attempt by the administration to change a part of the school system, and any suggestion that things will improve will be blunted by their immediate assumption that all will fail. This nihilistic pessimism is the result of their overwhelming experience that from their perspective validates this inference about the future. Finality in this context is a site of imperviability that needs to be made a topic of conversation. Conversing about finality will uncover the hidden experiences and feelings that create sites of imperviability to change.

The Institutionalization of Education

To broaden a discussion of change within educational systems requires the inclusion of an analysis of education as an institution. Sites of imperviability and sanctioned types of conversation become woven into the tightly controlled and aggressively defended structure of the institution. To properly contextualize the commentary of the participants about their experience requires a description of the educational bureaucracy of which they are a part. In addition, a critical examination of the participants' commentary requires the further recognition that teachers are members of a bureaucratic institution and targets of commercial and political interests, and their pedagogy is a complex combination of these influences and demands.

The participants' school is typically bureaucratic in its differentiation of space, time, and people. The day, the class periods, and the school year are punctuated by buzzers, bus schedules, and vacations, all of which reflect the systemic organization and values of the school. The school is organized into specialized activity areas such as physical education, music, art, science, math, home economics, administration, duplication of materials, etc. People are differentiated by age (kindergarten through twelfth grade; teachers and students) and by function (teachers, students, administrators, maintenance staff, cafeteria workers, clerical workers).

Why is this bureaucratic differentiation germane to the reflections of the participants? Because they are part of a highly organized, rigid institution focused on efficiently sustaining itself. Homogeneity and order are prized characteristics in a system that strives homeostatically for a steady state. The characteristics of the bureaucracy significantly affect the individual and collective construction of meaning. Whether deliberately or accidentally the hierarchy of authority, the division of labor, the rules and regulations, the impersonal orientation, and the routinized behavior provide the context for the knowledge production of the members of the bureaucracy.

The spatial structuring of schools affects the success of change initiatives. When school systems are geographically decentralized, with schools and administrative functions dispersed throughout a district, a "*loose coupling*" or structural looseness can occur (Bennett & LeCompte, 1990). The phenomenon of loose coupling can also occur within schools, and due to the inability of administration in hierarchically centralized systems to supervise teachers on a regular basis, "teachers need only close their doors to avoid surveillance" (Bennett & LeCompte, 1990, p. 57). However, the geographical dispersion and closed doors of the teachers are detrimental to the development of teacher collegiality and the organization of teacher opposition to administrative practices. Though the closed door phenomenon facilitates teacher autonomy by allowing teachers the freedom from administrative supervision to try new educational techniques, dispersion and "closed door autonomy" have a deleterious effect on change. Although they allow teachers to resist administratively promoted change (Bennett & LeCompte, 1990), the imposed isolation, individualization, and balkanization of the teachers (Hargreaves, 1994) does not promote collegial dialogue and reflection. Therefore, a collective construction of authentic and relevant change does not take place. Teachers who exist in a balkanized and individualized school culture are much more at the mercy of the bureaucracy than those in collaborative cultures who can form coalitions to promote change.

The intransigence of bureaucracies against change is reinforced by the refractory nature of teachers. Historically, teachers as individuals and faculties have maintained a teacher-centered mode of instruction and curriculum (Cuban 1993). Even when empowered, they generally resist change. Tanner and Tanner report a lesson learned about teacher autonomy:

> For any number of reasons teachers do not use the power they actually possess to improve the curriculum. Teachers generally see themselves as being fairly autonomous-as being in control of what is taught and how it is taught—but when it comes to actual practice, they tend to depart very little from a single approach: standing in front of a class—telling, explaining, or lecturing. Thus, although teachers make the curriculum, they are not using their autonomy to implement what they recognize as desirable educational practices. (1990, p. 308)

The political implications of post-formal conversation and the ubiquity of power in discussions of change require teachers to become aware of the institutional forces that affect their construction of meaning. The new direction in promoting educational change suggests that teachers cannot be truly autonomous until they examine these forces and interests in the context of the past and the present.

Conclusion

The earlier chapters showed how the failure of educational change is related to the use of modernistic techniques and strategies to solve postmodern problems. The problem of educational change is exacerbated by teacher cultures that are inherently resistant to change. Resolving this culturally oriented crisis requires a paradigm shift to a new direction entailing the development of the skills and knowledge contained in post-formal conversation, affect control theory, stakeholder empowerment, systemic thinking, and knowledge about the institutionalization of education. The new direction recognizes power as a central component of the problem and the solution. Another imperative is the development of schools as learning organizations characterized by post-formal conversation.

This research provided an opportunity for the participants and me to reflect and construct our meanings about our experiences with educational change. Now that the context has been fully developed, the participants' stories and the research story can be told.

Chapter Five

Teacher Talk: Post-Formal Stories

What is a post-formal story? What shape does it take, what tale does it tell? Obviously, there are no systematic, prescriptive answers to these questions. The answers differ with each story because of the idiosyncratic context constructed by the storytellers. In the case of *Teacher Talk*, the story varies from personal anecdotes to more formal analyzes of the participants' experience in relation to theory, deemed relevant by me, the researcher. Even though other post-formal stories take diverse forms, a post-formal story contains certain critical nontraditional perspectives.

One perspective is to recognize the different types of narratives that facilitate the understanding of our experience by acting as different lenses through which our experience can be examined. Laurel Richardson (1997) identifies five types of narratives that are instructive in our attempt to understand the nature of the post-formal story. Richardson identifies the everyday narrative (an examination of what we did today), the autobiographical narrative ("how people articulate how the past is related to the present"), the biographical narrative (understanding other people's lives; empathizing with the life stories of others), the cultural narrative (participating in the narratives of one's culture; understanding the cultural meanings and their relationships to one another), and the collective story (giving "voice to those who are silenced or marginalized in the cultural narrative") (1997, pp. 29–33).

Teacher Talk, being a post-formal story, contains a bit of all of Richardson's narrative types. Specifically, through the process of critical reflection, *Teacher Talk* contains parts of autobiographies, and through the post-formal conversation, biographical and collective narratives emerge. The understandings constructed by the participants (including the research story) occurred because the participants were able to link the events of their lives into a narrative (Polkinghorne, 1988). Identifying critical moments in our lives and temporally linking them, provides the larger context within which multiple and diverse processes can be used to discern the hidden patterns embedded within the narrative of our lives.

Another perspective that is characteristic of the post-formal story can be explained through the idea of "landscape" (Connelly & Clandinin, eds., 1999). Connelly and Clandinin (1999) utilize this metaphor in trying to understand teacher knowledge. They view the "professional knowledge landscape" metaphor as an opportunity to talk about "space, place, and time;" as an opportunity "filled with diverse people, things, and events in different relationships" (Clandinin & Connelly, 1995, eds. pp. 4–5). In addition, this metaphor provides the opportunity to see these relationships, not only in an intellectual perspective, but also in a moral and emotional perspective (Clandinin & Connelly, eds., 1995). The reintegration of emotion and intellect is an essential element of a post-formal story.

A final perspective is, simply that, post-formal stories are characterized by post-formal thinking. The post-formal story is informed by considerations of

- the origins of knowledge, or the understanding of "the etymology of the cultural forms embedded within us" (Kincheloe, 1993, p. 158);
- the hidden patterns of the deeper structure of reality (Bohm & Peat, 1987) that is not easily discernable through the use of modernistic processes (Kincheloe, 1998);
- the "integral reconceptualized post-formal processes [of] deconstruction, the connection of logic and emotion, and the transcendence of simple cause-effect to non-linear holism" (Horn, 1999, 1999b);
- the broad context of all of the story's components, including the most critical—considerations of power.

What follows are stories of the post-formal genre, in that post-formal thinking and post-formal conversation shaped the construction and telling of them.

The Research Story

Is post-formal inquiry a viable method in achieving the dual purposes of gaining knowledge about educational change and facilitating the critical transformation of the participants? This question will be answered first by reviewing the method as explicated in Chapter Two and then by discussing the outcomes of the research.

Interpretivist and Constructivist Ethnography

As detailed in Chapter Two, post-formal inquiry draws upon other types of qualitative inquiry as antecedents. My research was somewhat descriptively ethnographic, but it was more of an interpretivist and constructivist ethnography since the purpose of my presence was to participate in and facilitate the participants' description and construction of their experience. This participation and facilitation were achieved through a range of activities in which I was an active participant, not a neutral observer. In the individual and group interviews, my participation was evident in the formulation of follow-up questions, in my reactions to the other participants' individual and collectively constructed interpretations, and especially in my affective reactions to their emotions.

In the affective context, my participation was necessary to validate their emotional response to their reconstruction or interpretation of a prior experience. When Dave became frustrated and angry, I validated his affective state through my body language and verbal response because I felt that his emotions were a genuine (and critically important) part of his construction of meaning. For me to do otherwise would have been to separate the intellectual and affective components that made up his interpretation. Such a reductionist bifurcation of his integrated and genuine interpretation would have been intrusive, manipulative, and distortional. When emotion surfaced, I interpreted the integration of intellect and emotion as an indication that a more complex interpretation had been holistically generated by the research experience. Sue's emotion during her first interview indicated that the reflective conversation in which we were engaged challenged certain assumptions that were the basis for her interpretations of her efficacy. Her emotional display represented a pivotal point in her recognition of the systemic context of her assumptions about her professional self-esteem and in her subsequent reinterpretation of her professional efficacy.

At various times in their construction of meaning, each of the participants became intellectually engaged, emotionally engaged, or engaged in a construction containing both intellectual and emotional properties. The idea that emotion and intellect can be separated is a fallacy. Post-formal inquiry requires an acceptance that all human experience is characterized by the dynamic interaction of the intellect and emotion. This became apparent in Sue's first interview as described in Chapter Four.

In retrospect, I am not sure whether the valuable reflections and meanings about Sue's past experience and her professional efficacy would have been constructed without my sincere emotional and intellectual validation of her distress. The display of the affective component of her current meanings about her professional self created a leverage opportunity for me to insert the new possibility (theory) of isolation as a major causative component in her interpretation. Sue's processing of the isolation possibility and her open display of emotion led her to revisit her past experience in the new context of her enervating isolation.

Toward the end of the interview, Sue said that she felt better and was glad that we had kept talking. She continued her processing of the experience by saying, "I mean that it is a drastic change [becoming isolated]. It is like when you don't have any children, and all of a sudden you have a child. When you go from teaching most of your career in one kind of an environment, and then all of a sudden there you are with four walls around you and all those kids. And that's it. Then forever it is just you and those kids." She continued: "Only another teacher understands this. My husband doesn't understand this; a spouse can't get it. To understand, you have to go through this."

Sue's processing did not stop at the end of the interview, because at the next interview she was *affectively* a different person. In fact, she was once again the self-assured, efficacious individual who had somehow got lost over the years. Her aggressive processing of our experience in the first interview became evident in her heavily annotated feedback paper and her desire to start the interview by going through this paper. The importance of the feedback paper in facilitating her post-interview processing was obvious when, well into the second interview, she thumbed through the pages of the document and started us in a new direction with the comment: "But there is a whole section here on where do initiatives come from."

The activities that allowed my participation and facilitation of the participants' description and construction of their experience included the feedback papers, the exchange of transcripts, and the sharing of my journals. The feedback papers were researcher/participant interactive in that I selected the issues or commentary from the interview that would be the focus of the feedback; I created the opportunity to expand the interview conversation by asking questions, I decided what theory or additional information to include in the feedback; and I attempted to focus the reader's attention through the use of underlining and bold print. The exchange of transcripts created the opportunity to develop the individual conversations into group conversations, to disseminate the theory, and to engage the participants in theory and practice that might not have surfaced in their individual conversation. The sharing of my documentation (journals, glossary, chronology) was also a way to introduce my interpretations into the conversational mix. One intention of my activity in participants' interpretation of their experience was to broaden the conversation by introducing new ideas and challenging their constructions.

Critical Ethnography

Critical ethnography, with its focus on the historical, social, and economic context of power, was another antecedent of this post-formal inquiry. As will be seen in the participants' stories, the ubiquity of power manifested itself in participants' comments on their relationship with other stakeholders such as administrators and students. Issues of power were confined to the participants' position in the hierarchical arrangement of their school system and did not include manifestations of power in areas like race and gender. Power in the context of age did not emerge except in the sense of teachers-as-adults and students-as-children. The young teacher/old teacher issue was more of a cultural concern in the context of the alienation induced by the balkanized and individualized school culture.

As the participant-researcher, I concluded that the sole focus of power was on the hegemonic, hierarchical structure of the school. I based this upon my interpretation that the amount of power they held in their school revealed itself as the primary concern of Barry, Dave and Steve; it was also related to Sue's isolation. As will be shown later in this chapter, Dan's acknowledgment of his uncontested power in his classroom was more important to him then his decision-making power outside his classroom. This led to my supposition that people must resolve their most important concerns before they can consider other concerns. Given the intensity and tenaciousness of their concern with the issue of power in their professional lives, it would be difficult for these participants to seriously and critically engage issues of student empowerment, race, or gender without first resolving their own empowerment issues. Consequently, any attempt by me to direct their critical attention to other areas of a lower priority to them would have endangered the authentic relationship being fostered. Also, my supposition might help explain their collective resistance to theory, which will be examined later in this chapter. The participants reported that in their professional lives the theory they encountered had no relevance to their actual practice or professional needs. Consequently, they devalued the theory that was presented to them and relied upon their experience to generate the theoretical basis for their practice and beliefs. The issue of inauthentic and irrelevant theory being forced on the participants also relates to the development of trustworthiness.

Trustworthiness

Trustworthiness is apparent when the researcher and the participants work together to construct, critically reflect upon, and reconstruct an understanding of the past, present, and future. The achievement of trustworthiness is evident when the participants and the researcher perceive each other as equal. The researcher must not be perceived as holding interpretive power over the participants, and all must engage in reshaping their cognitive structures to accommodate the new information and new contexts uncovered by their problem solving and critically reflective thinking.

In Chapter Two, I suggested that in an educational context, anticipatory accommodation (the reshaping of the cognitive processes used in constructing meaning) would be evident when teachers, who prior to the inquiry did not include concepts such as power, systems thinking, teacher culture, conversational types, and affect control theory in their construction of meaning, now included these concepts. Participants' anticipatory accommodation could be used as the criterion to determine the degree of trustworthiness that developed in this research.

In this research, the participants sporadically used or alluded to the theoretical terminology that I introduced. Yet there was no continuous reference to or overt use of the ideas. What did occur was a sincere continuous participation in the research and a willingness to engage in frank, intimate conversation about important personal issues. This kind of conversation requires a sense of trust and safety that allows the open examination of one's interpretations of the past, present, and, future. The egalitarian and trustworthy relationship led to a reshaping of cognitive structures through critical reflection on professional experience. Examples of the reshaping of participants' cognitive structures will be seen later in Sue's change in her professional self-perception and in Barry's acceptance of the possibility of including administrators in conversations about change. As previously discussed, the criticality of the reshaping of their cognitive structures was limited to issues of power that personally affected the participants. However, this first step in their critical inquiry was made possible by the safe space mutually created by the researcher, the participants themselves, and the research method.

Hegemonic power and types of teacher culture became the theoretical constructs most frequently included in the conversations. As will be seen in their stories, all the participants used the teacher culture information in interpreting their experience, and all recognized the effect of power in the formation of their professional experience. Participants frequently mentioned dialogue and dialectical conversation. However, they referred infrequently to systems theory. They did not talk about their emotions, but they became emotional. The relationships between the participants and the researcher achieved a state of equality and safety that allowed emotion to be displayed. This above all was the best indicator of trustworthiness.

Resistance Postmodernism
As stated in Chapter Two, one goal of my research was to "challenge dominant Western research practices that are underwritten by a foundational epistemology and a claim to universally valid knowledge at the expense of local, subjugated knowledges" (Kincheloe & McLaren, 1994, p. 153). Generally, an expert who is value-neutral quantitatively drives dominant Western research practices. In this case, I was a participant observer utilizing qualitative methodology.

This research posed an additional challenge to the dominant professional development strategies currently utilized by schools. Generally, teachers are not researchers. Instead, they engage in tightly controlled reductionist-transmissional activities, not in educational research of a resistance postmodern nature. In instances when teachers engage in action research, they do so in a reductionist manner. They concentrate on one aspect of their craft or curriculum such as student assessment, classroom management, or the infusion of technology to their courses. In a postmodern resistance project, teachers would be allowed to set the direction of the research and reflectively, through collegial conversation, explore the core issues of education as identified and described by them. The issues that are identified as "core" issues do not deal with perfunctory aspects of curriculum and instruction (writing programs, content, student assessment) but with the issues that directly affect their professional lives and environment (power, autonomy, participation in decision making). In this project, teachers did not engage in perfunctory action research. The conversation with each other and with me was about power, autonomy, and their participation (or lack of participation) in decisions that affected their professional lives.

The research practice and the professional development strategy utilized by this research did not promote a foundational epistemology, nor did it claim to promote universally valid knowledge. Instead, it was constructivist in promoting critical reflection on the participants' experience, from which they constructed relevant and authentic meanings. The research practice and professional development strategies used in this research recognize the local and interactive nature of knowledge production. Another significant component of this research, which is generally avoided in traditional educational research and professional development, was the recognition and acceptance of emotion. In my experience, most contemporary professional development strives to avoid delving into the emotional, for that is uncharted ground, rife with unpredictability.

Catalytic Inquiry
Did this method reorient, focus, and energize the participants toward knowing their reality in order to transform it? Certainly Sue's experience suggests a reorientation in two ways: her resolution of her feelings of professional inadequacy and her promotion of collegial conversation. The rest of the participants were inarguably focused on issues of power within the educational hierarchy of which they were a part. Do they now know their reality in a way that will cause them to attempt to transform it? They did take one step, that is, to incorporate dialogic conversation in their in-service opportunities. Whether further steps will be taken toward a resolution of their power issues and an exploration of student empowerment remain to be seen. Without the catalyst of the researcher's activity, in light of the system's resistance to this sort of critical activity, and in light of the participants' career stage, the probability of further significant action is low. However, while engaged in a method they found helpful, they were momentarily empowered and motivated to continue the conversation.

Collegial Collaboration
My two biggest surprises in this research initiative were the intensity of emotion and personal feelings disclosed during the conversations and the participants' unwillingness to end conversations. In almost all cases, regardless of the time pressure imposed by other obligations, the participants wanted to keep talking. "Conversational overrun" was the norm. In most of the transcripts there are one or two places where I formally indicate that the conversation is over, and these comments are followed by an additional five to ten pages of transcribed conversation. I quickly learned not to turn off the tape recorders when I talked about ending the interview. My conjecture as to the reason for this phenomenon is that the participants were hungry for this kind of experience. Through the interviews, it became apparent that the opportunity for professional dialogic conversation was rare. Throughout the study, I sensed the participants' agreement that this work constituted a *collaborative* effort by *colleagues* to better understand our experiences with educational change. The participants' willingness to converse with each other and their extension of dialogic conversation to the rest of the faculty through their in-service proposal supported my premise.

The participants' sense of collegiality was evident in the group conversation. At the beginning of the group conversation, I asked each of the participants to identify themselves and state what they taught, how many years of experience they had, and what they thought of this type of conversation. The following are their comments:

> Barry: I have enjoyed the conversations that Ray and I have had. It has brought back some memories and some angers and frustrations. It has really been very interesting, and as far as group conversation is concerned I thought it would be a neat thing to sit down with the other participants and hear what they have to say and to exchange ideas.
>
> Dan: I like the type of presentation because I think it is something that is real. It is not something that is an artificial kind of presentation. I wanted to become involved in the group conversation because I want to hear what the other people have to say. I am sure there will be some ideas that I would gain from having been a part of these conversations.
>
> Steve: When Ray originally asked me to be a part of the project, I agreed because it sounded interesting. I will just echo what everyone else has said. I am looking forward to hearing what other people have to say, and to sharing experiences.
>
> Barry: I would like to say how much I enjoyed conversing on the things that we have. It was kind of neat going back and remembering how things were, and how they turned out—how we got to this point. It was great to relive the experiences that we shared, and I enjoyed reading the other people's comments.

Collegial collaboration was promoted by all of the participants. Undoubtedly, this occurred because, instead of an I-It relationship between the researcher and the subject, an I-Thou relationship was established between the researcher and the other participants.

A Description of the Conversation

The conversation in all of its manifestations occurred over a seven-month period. Barry and Sue each had two formal individual interviews, whereas Dan, Dave, and Steve each had one. A transcript of each taped interview was made, and a feedback paper followed each interview. There was one formal group conversation; this included all of the participants except Dave. There were other times when some participants would informally converse about the research study and issues raised in the conversations. Transcripts and feedback papers were also generated for the group conversation. I distributed all my journals, including the conversation chronology and the glossary of theory, to the participants prior to the group conversation. I held a debriefing conversation with each participant after each one had received the transcript and feedback paper, and each person participated in member-checking the parts of this study that included that person's participation. The formal individual interviews and the group conversation were approximately one and a half to two hours in length. The debriefing conversations were approximately forty-five minutes to one hour in length.

There were numerous informal conversations, configured in various ways. I participated in some of the conversations, and other conversations included only some of the participants. These ranged from short hallway conversations to more lengthy faculty-room exchanges. I first became aware of the conversations between the participants when, early on, Barry and Dave mentioned in their individual interviews and to me in informal conversation that they would like to read each other's transcripts and have a group conversation.

The blurring of boundaries led to another phenomenon that is worthy of attention. Because of the nature (collegial collaboration and trustworthiness) and content of the type of conversations in which we were engaged, the same issues and feelings that emerged in the research conversations began to surface in conversations about issues arising from our daily routines. For instance, after a faculty meeting or a curriculum committee meeting, I was able to point out examples of theory, previously introduced in our research, that had arisen during the meeting. For instance, the administrative techniques used to tightly control faculty meetings became obvious to the participants. The nature and content of our research conversation consciously and unconsciously informed our teachers' union activity. Power structures and community building took on added importance when the union leadership, which included two of the participants, assessed situations. Current issues such as union activity, school discipline concerns, in-service concerns, current change initiatives, our relationship with the administration, and our isolation as teachers became the objects in our research conversation around which we explored theory and experience. Perhaps the focus on current issues is another reason why the critical focus of this research was more on power and culture than on race, gender, or student empowerment.

The action taken by the participants to gain in-service time for collegial conversation formed another conversational strand. Steve, Sue, and myself held a formal meeting in which we developed a game plan to achieve this goal. Ensuing conversations were held with three other faculty members who were not part of the research group. These conversations led to one of the nonmembers of the research group making a successful presentation of our proposal to a faculty advisory committee and to the principal, leading to an agreement by the committee and the principal to include in-service time for faculty dialogic conversation during the next school year.

As discussed later in this chapter, because of the exigencies and obligations of our daily routine, there were times when not everyone could be part of a conversational opportunity. This resulted in shorter conversations between various people, in which one person would "fill in" the person who had been unable to attend. The conversational opportunities were diverse in relation to the participants, and to duration, form (individual, group, written), and to intent (reflecting, problem solving, informing, or venting emotions). The aspects of conversation experienced by my research group are elements of a post-formal conversation.

Interview Format and Sequence
As detailed in Chapter Two, each of the interviews started with general questions, and the follow-up questions were based on the commentary of the participants and my agenda. My original plan was to provide as little input into the participants' construction of their experience as possible, so as not to prejudice their thinking. This would allow a comparison between their constructions of meaning before interacting with the others and their constructions after interacting. Of course, this initial attempt to remain somewhat neutral was quickly offset by my catalytic intent as enacted through the follow-up questions and the commentary I provided in my questioning. For instance, in Barry's second individual interview I posed a general question about how educational change affected his professional life. His reply centered on the cyclic, faddish nature of change. This response was followed by my question: "Do you see differences between your earlier years as a teacher versus now?" He replied that the relationships between all professionals (teachers and administrators) had been more collegial in the past, but they had changed to a more rigid, hierarchical system. With that, I read an excerpt from the first interview. "In our first interview you made a comment to the effect that your school system seems to be a top-down hierarchical system with decentralized power. You also said that in the earlier years 'because I was a professional, we were equals.' Does that mean that the system was more collegial or egalitarian in the past?" Barry then confirmed his earlier interpretation and justified it with an additional comment about a lack of respect from the top down that bred a lack of respect from the bottom up.

This reiteration of his prior comment reinforced Barry's interpretation of the past and present as being different, in terms of the relationships between administration and teachers and the change in decision-making power. Would he have felt as strongly about this interpretation without my reiteration? This interpretation became more concrete in both of our minds when I confirmed it in my next question. "Okay, why did it change? How would you pinpoint the reason for the change?" At this point we both accepted the interpretation as a factual basis for a significant part of the ensuing conversation, if not for the duration of the research. Barry followed my question with the speculation that it might have been a generational matter, and he provided details about each of the administrators from then to now. My next question forced him to make a value judgment. "Okay, which way do you prefer?" Barry's reply: "The old way." My follow-up question: "Why?"

From this point in the conversation, the issue of difference between the early years and the present became a main theme in Barry's understanding of his past and present experience. How involved was I in the development of this theme? The answer to this question would be difficult to ascertain. Fortunately, it is not as important as the fact that through our interaction, this interpretation was accepted as a fact by both of us, as well as by the others who read the transcripts and participated in the later group discussions. This conversational sequence is an example of how socially constructed meaning arises through the process of post-formal conversation.

Another realization, important to understanding how Barry and I constructed an interpretation of the difference between the early years and the current years, is that I had a critical agenda that I wanted to promote. The interpretation that Barry and I constructed presented a perfect opportunity to promote one aspect of my critical agenda—the issue of power. In the same sequence of conversation, in relation to a former superintendent of schools, Barry had mentioned power. I noted that reference and later focused the conversation directly on the issue of power. "You brought up the issue of power. Who should have power in the school? Everyone, or only some? Should there be an 'administrative power' separate from a 'classroom teacher power'?" After two comments by Barry, I returned to the issue of power. "Okay, let's talk about power in the context of decision making—decision making about things like curriculum, instruction, discipline, assessment, block scheduling. Who should be making the decisions on that?" My consistent focus on power produced a three-fold effect. First, it forced Barry to expand his interpretation of the difference between the early and the current years to include a consideration of power. Second, it further strengthened Barry's interpretation by providing additional proof of the difference. Third, his response legitimized and reinforced my critical agenda—an agenda significantly based on unequal distributions of power.

The interview format and sequence of questions played out as interactive conversation, during which the participants enjoyed a degree of latitude in charting the general course. However, to a degree I steered the conversation toward an accommodation of my agenda as previously revealed in the discussion of my research methodology and theory.

Transcripts and Feedback Papers
The transcripts were valuable in the promoting of reflection on what had been said. People were eager to read about what they had said. Their reading not only provided an opportunity to confirm or deny their initial interpretations and to elaborate on the interpretations they wished to sustain, it also reinforced the information that I introduced through my questioning and my commentary.

Another benefit of transcribing and disseminating the conversation was that it set the stage for the later collective conversation. In my journals I noted that, early on, all participants were eager to read each other's transcripts and that I was amazed at the intensity of the personal reflections in terms of emotion and disclosure of personal feelings. The participants' willingness to share transcripts and give personal commentary provided a context of intimacy that enhanced the collegiality of the group conversations. This strong affective component of their commentary also enhanced the trustworthiness of my method and the trustworthiness of their relationship with each other and me. Their desire to continue the conversation as a group, together with the continuation of the personal nature of their disclosures to each other, further suggests this enhanced trustworthiness.

Originally, the purpose of the feedback papers was to introduce theory into the conversation. My hope was that the feedback papers would help participants to develop a common critical language, facilitate their empowerment through the attainment of knowledge, and provide a theoretical basis for their reflections on their experience and current situation. I found that the theoretical terms participants most used were those that most aptly described the experiences they were reporting and their interpretations of their experience. For example, they all used the term "balkanized" in their conversations because it precisely conveyed a condition of their culture that they all recognized. Also, they were all able to distinguish between "dialogue" and "dialectical" conversation. They applied their knowledge to our impromptu and formal conversations after faculty meetings about the type of conversation allowed by the principal (predominantly dialectic and discussion).

The feedback papers were also valuable as a "catching up" device for members of the conversation group who had not started with the others. Because of his fall coaching activities, Dave was not able to participate in his first interview until long after some of the others. Also, during the first semester Steve was involved in a theatrical production and likewise started his participation at a much later date. With everyone else's permission, when Steve and Dave were ready to begin, they received all the transcripts and feedback papers. Since the paper blitz could be overwhelming, the feedback papers delivered a concise and summative way to get into the flow. They also guaranteed a repetitive reading of the theory and the main interpretations of the other participants. The repetition of ideas is evident in the feedback paper for Barry concerning his second individual interview (see Appendix D). In comments two and five I encouraged him to reflect on a prior assumption by reiterating what he had earlier constructed, and I provided an opportunity for him to critically reflect on his interpretation by following the reiteration with new questions aimed at extending the conversation.

Debriefings and Member Checking

Debriefings and member checking were two somewhat interchangeable activities. In both activities, the participants received an opportunity to review any material relating to their participation in this research. This included any conversational segments relating to them and the story written about them (for which see later in this chapter). The subtle difference was that the debriefings involved a final reflection on participants' interpretations about their educational experience, while member checking simply checked the accuracy of what they had said. Essentially, the primary function of both activities was checking for accuracy. However, these activities also provided another opportunity for me to challenge participants' reflections and interject theory into the conversation, which in turn, I hope, expanded their awareness of their experience.

Member checking consisted of giving copies of relevant parts of the research paper to each participant and having each one either approve what was written or rewrite it. On the surface this appears to be a perfunctory chore. However, it provided one more opportunity for the participants to reflect on their interpretations. Sue chose to write her responses, while the rest preferred the taped interview format.

The debriefing was essentially a closure activity with multiple purposes (see Appendix A). Besides providing an opportunity for the participants to critique some of my conclusions, it also introduced new information to the participants (see the "Spiritual Crisis" section in Chapter Three). In addition, I was once again able to direct the participants' focus toward issues relevant to my agenda. Also, both activities served the purpose of giving formal closure to this research study. Therefore, what came of these activities? Did each person respond to the questions? As explained in Chapter Two, the participants generally felt that the questions broadened the conversation, but the lack of time available for this type of critical reflection severely limited the potential of the questioning technique.

The Teacher's View of Change
Part of the research story is the participants' view of educational change, specifically through their stories. Generally, they agreed with the criticisms of American education as previously presented. They agreed that educational change is cyclic, trendy, politically influenced, and expert driven, as well as with the exigencies wrought by the collision of the modern and the postmodern. Their recollections represented the crumbling mission and educational obsolescence of modern education.

The participants shared enough experience to permit a fairly common narrative about their experience yet still leave space for idiosyncratic interpretations. Emotionally, they were all frustrated and contentious in their remembrances; however, Barry and Dan's anger and hostility were more sharply directed at the administration, whereas Sue's was more inward and personal. Views of change also revealed idiosyncratic interpretations. Dan's view of change differed from that of the others in that his construction of meaning was focused tightly on curriculum and instruction, whereas Barry, Dave, and Sue directed their view of change more toward culture and power. Steve's narrative combined elements of both culture and power, and curriculum and instruction. However, despite this disparity of focus, Dan's final story included a recognition of the meanings that were important to the others, although even this inclusion of culture and power in his story was overshadowed by his own interpretations.

In the debriefing, Dan alluded to the isolation that resulted from the collapse of the open space into the balkanized departments and isolated, self-contained classrooms. (These ideas resulted from interactions with the others and from my introduction of theory). However, he contextualized this fact within his own interpretive construct (his tight focus on the curriculum and the instruction he controls in his classes) by pointing out that he likes being isolated because it affords him power over his pedagogy. We see this in the following exchange:

Dan: I think that the way the building is now designed does promote more isolation, but I don't mind that because I feel there are times that I can do things that I otherwise couldn't.

Ray: Some of the other teachers see power, and their perceived lack of empowerment, as important to them. I would guess that you always felt empowered. When you go into your classroom, as far as curriculum, instruction, and classroom management is concerned, you have all of the power that you need or want. Is that a correct assessment?

Dan: Yes that is correct. Maybe I don't want as much as some people do. I like the way that you said it; I feel that I have as much as I need and want at this point. I never really felt that I was inhibited in doing what I really wanted to do in class. I honestly don't know of any time in my whole thirty-nine years that I was told you must teach a certain thing, or a certain way.

Constraints on This Post-Formal Process

This inquiry could be criticized on the grounds that we accomplished nothing concrete. No new courses of study were written, no new teaching strategies were implemented, and no solutions to any of the postmodern problems previously identified were found. This criticism is valid if the study is viewed in a modernistic context that values empirical, measurable change: a context in which professional development is reductionistic, and a quick fix syndrome predominates. Post-formal professional development is not quick-fix or reductionist; it is a holistic, systemic process that values the egalitarian participation of all stakeholders in establishing egalitarian communities that can meet the challenges of a postmodern society. Essentially, this research is a snapshot of one segment of an on-going, ever-evolving process. Because it is a process, the relevant questions include the following: How could this process have been better facilitated? How can this process become an on-going part of the professional development of all teachers in the school?

The participants reported their problem with time: the lack of available time to reflect. These comments lead us not only to a major constraint on post-formal professional development but also to a major difference between modernistic and post-formal professional development. Modernistic professional development can be packaged to accommodate any time constraints imposed by the school. The expansion and compaction qualities of modernistic professional development accommodate day-long or short after-school in-services. Since accommodation of time in a modernistic context is of the utmost importance, continuity and authenticity are sacrificed. The inauthenticity produced by time accommodation is another reason why many teachers feel that in-service programs fail to meet their needs.

Post-formal professional development is not only extremely time sensitive, but also to some degree incompatible with existing in-service schedules. The emotional and personal aspects of this process require a continuity that is not accommodated by the current time structures. However, my research does show an inherent resiliency in post-formal conversation, in relation to the obstacles that arose. The conclusion we all drew was that regular time has to be allocated during the school day, or on some kind of regular basis, for this kind of professional development.

The original intent of this research was to conduct a continuous conversation devoid of long periods of inactivity. I feared that if gaps in the conversation occurred, interest would wane, and the critical continuity would be lost. The ideal was to construct a segue concerning some issue consisting of individual interviews, feedback papers, group conversations, feedback papers, and perhaps collegial and collective action taken. Instead, reality impinged on this plan. Meeting times became problematic because of real-world conditions such as Sue's children playing fall and winter sports, which greatly reduced her availability. Barry's child played a sport; Steve was in a theatrical production; Dave coached a fall sport, took two trips, and coached a spring sport; Dan had a number of medical emergencies in his family; and we all had other school-related meetings after school. In addition to this, Barry had to leave school for approximately two months due to unexpected surgery.

To further complicate our continuous conversation, I assumed the responsibility for caring for my grandmother, who was diagnosed with Alzheimer's disease. My responsibility to my grandmother, which began early in the research process and continued throughout it, proved to be enervating as well as time consuming. In short, participating in this research proved to be a challenge; however, all the participants found the post-formal process motivating enough to steadfastly continue their participation. The constraints proved beneficial in that they provided a severe test of the attractiveness and resiliency of the method. Also, they led to the discovery of the important fact that post-formal professional development requires dedicated time.

One obvious conclusion is that if a school is committed to community building of this nature, then time must be secured for post-formal activities. On the other hand, if teachers unilaterally wish to promote community building through this process, then they must appropriate time during the professional day and create time outside of the professional day to engage in this process. Whether during or after the school day, using time for this process is an act of resistance to the modernistic attitudes and structures that are impervious to change. A direct consequence of adopting this type of professional development is the necessity of embracing a holistic, systemwide approach, which is a requirement for the implementation of large-scale post-formal professional development.

What is the Potential of Post-Formal Inquiry?
Finally, what is the potential of post-formal inquiry as a postmodern professional development model? An attempt to answer this question generates other questions that are the essence of post-formal inquiry. Can a post-formal conversation that includes all stakeholders be cultivated? Is there a time commitment to converse, to reflect, to engage theory? Can the stakeholders broaden their perspective by developing a systemic view? Will this effort lead to a shared vision? Will the stakeholders commit themselves to building a community? Can a spirituality be fostered that will coalesce into a transcendent, motivating phenomenon? All these questions need to be addressed because post-formal inquiry, like the world in which we exist, is a holistic, integrated entity that defies reduction. This does not mean that reductionism and systematic actions are not valuable. It means that for them to be valuable they need to be developed in the context of their effects on the whole system. Post-formal inquiry, if employed in the manner described in this research, is a process that will guarantee complexity and provide for the authentic use of a diversity of actions that will accommodate the exigencies of the postmodern condition.

The potential of post-formal inquiry was shown in the willingness of the participants to converse collegially, and to seek to extend the conversation to their peers. As Barry indicated, a necessary condition for resolving education's problems is the inclusion of the administration in this conversation. Can other stakeholders be included? In my opinion, this depends on the initial success of the conversation among teachers and administrators that will, I hope, focus on the formation of an egalitarian community.

In the short time in which they engaged in post-formal conversation, the participants projected a nascent disposition toward shared vision and the development of a spiritual commitment. Their disposition was evident in their willingness to share their intimate professional thoughts, in their mutual agreement concerning the importance of the vision and commitment of the early years, and in their agreement to pursue dialogic conversation with other faculty members. Given time to engage in post-formal conversation, these people could realize the potential of post-formal inquiry.

The Participants' Stories

Why tell the participants' stories as individual stories? An important aspect of post-formalism is the valuing of difference. In this case, difference is manifested as the individual identities of these educators. Each of their stories is unique because these stories represent people as individuals, not as an essentialized or generalized group. Just as post-formal inquiry recognizes the holistic nature of reality, so too it recognizes the particularity of reality, in this case addressed by providing the opportunity for each participant to be heard.

Once I wrote the "stories" section of this chapter, I gave all the individual participants an opportunity to change in any way what I had written about them. The ultimate ownership of each person's story belonged to that person. The participants' stories are told in order to honor their dedication to the welfare of others and the improvement of education.

Contextualizing Their Stories

Developing a root definition (Checkland & Scholes, 1990) of the purpose of the participants' educational system will further contextualize the participants' stories and explicate post-formalism. Banathy specifies that a root definition defines (1) the customers, the users of the system; (2) the actors who serve the system and accomplish the transformation process; (3) the transformation process, which processes and transforms the input into output; (4) a worldview, which makes the transformation meaningful in context; (5) the owners of the system, who are also owners of the design process; and (6) the environment, the entities outside of the system that are given or are to be defined (1996b, p. 136).

A modernistic root definition for an educational system, like the one to which the participants belong, would include the following: (1) the customers are children who need to be taught; (2) the actors are the administrators and teachers who provide learning experiences; (3) transformation involves role differentiation (administration, teachers, other adults) in teaching and managing students through a systematic and organized process; (4) the education and management of the students is the responsibility of the adults; (5) the owners are the administrators, the teachers, and possibly some parents; and (6) the environment is the school.

In contrast, a post-formal root definition as proposed by this research include the following: (1) the customers are adults and children together in a learning community; (2) the actors are all the people in the learning community, including external organizations and individuals who have input into the community (textbook publishers, media, professional development providers, government agencies); (3) transformation involves all stakeholders functioning as lifelong learners and collaborators in improving the physical, mental, emotional, and spiritual wellness of all people; (4) the primary responsibility for the welfare of the community lies with all the stakeholders; (5) the owners are all the stakeholders in the community; and (6) the environment is the entire school community and beyond.

These root definitions provide an additional backdrop for the stories of the participants. In addition, they can be applied to the participants' stories, providing a degree of continuity to allow the individual stories to synergistically paint a larger picture. In other words, as the stories of these career teachers and the history of education in their school has unfolded and is concluded with the telling of their individual tales, comparing their stories to the modernistic and post-formal root definitions will facilitate an understanding of post-formalism and an understanding of the position of the participants in this context.

A Description of the Participants' Educational Environment

As reported, our high school is culturally balkanized and individualized, with change initiatives characterized by contrived collegiality. Instances of collegial collaboration do occur, but they are short in duration, infrequent in occurrence, and not part of the system's modernistic root definition. Administrative culture is traditionally modernistic, with sharp boundaries between administrators and other stakeholders. This territoriality is compatible with the hierarchical arrangement of the stakeholders, with power centralized in the administrative level, though others are given limited power for specified tasks and durations.

In environmental structure, the participants' classrooms reflect their pedagogical philosophy. Desks are traditionally arranged in rows for primary learning activities, and students move these desks into small-group configurations when they engage in small-group work. When technology is available, students move to computer stations or computer laboratories. The library is another place where students are taken or can go for research purposes. However, the students always return to their original configuration of straight rows in classrooms. This environmental structure offers a powerful statement about teacher centeredness and control.

Individual teachers have significant control over the curricular content and instruction within their individual classrooms. The link between the taught curriculum and the formal curriculum is tenuous. The official paper curriculum is often written in general terms that allow teachers of the same subject free rein to develop differing activities. Often the only similarity in curriculum and instruction between different teachers' versions of the same course is the textbook and the general content area. The principal pointedly referred to this loosely coupled curriculum during a recent faculty meeting. Stung by faculty criticism that there was a deleterious inconsistency between the principal's and the assistant principal's enforcement of discipline, the principal defended his need for flexibility in interpreting and enforcing the written regulations by referring to the loose coupling of curriculum and instruction. He pointed out that the teachers see the value of not having rigid curricular and instructional procedures so that members of one department can go in many different directions in order to accommodate their individual curriculum and instructional preferences. Implying that the situation could be otherwise, he added that the faculty should understand the principal's need for equal flexibility in administering discipline.

Consequently, administrative supervision of the teachers is predominantly concerned with issues of student control and with public relations issues generated by students and parents about the classroom instruction of a particular teacher. If a teachers shows good classroom control, and no one complains about their pedagogy, the teachers are left alone. With regard to the instructional practices of the teachers, supervision is formalistic; administrators focus on teaching strategies mostly based on Madeline Hunter's effective teaching (1982) and Robert L. Canady's strategies for teaching in a block schedule (1995). A typical lesson is supposed to have an opening (an anticipatory set), a variety of activities (so that students are active, not bored), and some sort of closure. This formula is to be applied regardless of the learning activity.

Therefore, the school in which the participants teach is a traditionally modern school. Another accurate descriptor of this school system is a modification of Bela H. Banathy's paradigm (1996b) of the "old" and "new" story of organizational change (see Appendix E). The participants are unfortunately stuck in the "old story," but post-formal conversation is a means to move from the "old story" to the "new."

Barry's Story

The emotions that surfaced during the conversations with Barry are the key to understanding the focus of his story. This excerpt from his debriefing interview is a typical representation of Barry's affective interpretation of his experience:

> Barry: The emotions that I experienced at various times throughout the conversation went the full gamut from elation to sadness, depression and dejection. As you and I talked and as we talked at the roundtable [the group conversation] it was a positive reinforcement to hear that others shared similar feelings, but it was also a downer. It was depressing to see what could have been and what we now have. Are the emotions that I am experiencing at this point in my career similar or different from the emotions at other times of my career? I guess at this point they are less positive and more negative, whereas earlier in my career I would say they were the opposite. It used to be invigorating, challenging, and exciting to go in each day and to work with young people and to see them gain from the experience. Today it is not as rewarding. It is not as fulfilling, and I think the reason for that is the varied reasons that we have talked about throughout this project. They range from the administration to the kids themselves, and to theoretical things—a whole wide gamut of reasons why it is more negative than positive. In the other days there were so many positive emotions to get you to come to work every day. To work with kids because you could actually see that what you were accomplishing was benefiting the young person. You got support from the administration. Everything was built on a positive manner. Today you don't see that same success with each kid, and the relationship between faculty and administration has become more negatively oriented.
>
> Barry: I really enjoyed my involvement in this project. I enjoyed talking with you, with my colleagues, and the reflections that we had—the reminiscences that we had about how things used to be. I think as I look back over the first twenty-five years of my career and see all the positive things that occurred and how enjoyable it was, it makes the last part of my career a little more difficult to handle. It would have been nice to finish on the same positive note.

Barry's emotional response is linked to the change in his relationships with others. The primary focus that drives his meaning-making is centered on relationships. Throughout the dialogue he continuously returns to relationships—between teachers, administrators, and students, as well as different types of relationships, such as departmental, interdisciplinary, and social. When asked if at this point in his career he would prefer working in a team situation or remain isolated he responded:

> Well I would prefer a combination. I enjoy my autonomy in my classroom, but I also enjoyed the interaction and the exchanges that occurred in the open classroom. I think that in the open classroom you were able to achieve a degree of autonomy because you interacted when it was necessary—when you had a need. Also, other people didn't intrude on your space when you needed that autonomy.

This interpretation surfaced again in another interview:

> I think the English department in the open area used to converse a lot, share ideas, make suggestions, and interact. This no longer occurs because of the change in the structure. I think that we are ready to be put back into an open area.

Conversing, sharing, and interacting are more than attractive to Barry; they are central to his construction of meaning about his educational experience. The following comment indicates his strong need and desire for collegiality:

> Barry: As you were talking, a couple of ideas came to mind and I quickly jotted them down. I almost get the feeling that we're like the Stephen King novel whereby the vast majority of society is wiped out by the plague and there's a guy coming from Seattle, Washington; from Bangor, Maine; from Tallahassee, Florida; from Abilene, Texas. And they're kind of on a pilgrimage and they don't really know why they're doing it, or exactly where they're headed, but down the road they're going to come together in Las Vegas. It's like we are on a pilgrimage, kind of groping for a reuniting, a common sharing. I talked to Dave yesterday, and he expressed to me again the interest in reading other people's comments, an interest which I share and would love to do. Also he and I talked about a culminating activity—a roundtable activity that I think would really be a great catharsis at the end, whereby we talk about these things, and by hearing other people's recollections new things can be stirred from it. I certainly would be willing to share my ideas with whoever wanted them. I think a roundtable discussion for all the participants would really be a great closing activity.

Barry's emotional focus on relationships has been affected by his school culture, the type of conversation in his school, the lack of a systemic view, and the need for spirituality. These environmental factors significantly affected the following aspects of Barry's professional life: control of his classroom; his root definition of his professional life; his construction of meaning; and his spiritual condition. Being in a school system characterized by a culture of isolation provided limited opportunities for dialogic conversation, which resulted in a narrow view of the system. Since the driving force of the spiritual component of Barry's professional life involved interaction with others, the empowering motivation derived from a spiritual commitment was degraded along with his emotional state. His root definition changed from an egalitarian, community-oriented one to a modernistic definition of the purpose of schools. Since his professional world shrank to the limits of his classroom, his determination of what was important became narrowly focused on control of his class and on control of the boundaries between his small subsystem and the rest of the professional environment. These are the conditions that affected his construction of professional meanings and his interpretation of his experience.

In Barry's interpretations of his experience, five themes became apparent. The first theme was his insistence that there was a difference in attitude and viewpoint between the less experienced and the more experienced teachers. This part of his story was affected by his inability to form interpersonal relationships with the less experienced. The balkanization and individualization promoted a systemic barrier between these people, and conversational opportunities were tightly controlled because the administration viewed dialogic conversation as a threat to the status quo that they wished to maintain. The warm feelings that Barry remembered having for his colleagues of all ages in the earlier years could not be replicated with new colleagues in the current climate of isolation.

Another theme was the students' lack of responsibility as a major factor in the failure of education. As Barry said:

> Steve hit the nail on the head with the idea of responsibility; kids don't want to be responsible. They are capable of being responsible, it is just that they don't want to be bothered with responsibility. I'll tell you what stops me from doing a better job: it is the kids' unwillingness to work. Just think what it would be like if the kids were really into it. Just think of all of the neat things that you could do, and the things that you could teach them.

This part of Barry's story was predictable because of the lack of systemic awareness fostered by his isolation. Since his contact with other aspects of the total system was greatly reduced by his isolation and his lack of involvement in a collegial culture, Barry's focus had to be directed toward the only people with whom he had daily contact—the students. This narrowing of systemic awareness heightens the agency and individual power of the students. It is easier to blame them for their inability to achieve. Without sufficient contact with the total system, critical questions concerning power not only are never answered but are never asked. Placing undue focus exclusively on other stakeholders is the direct outcome of a culture of isolation that restricts stakeholder conversation.

A third theme was the need for standards. Once again, this hard-line attitude is a direct result of the pervasive isolation in Barry's school. Like the others, Barry was masterful in establishing an efficient, well-controlled classroom environment. In Barry's case, this was quite an achievement because he exclusively taught the "low sections," the least-desirable or less-skilled students. His security in believing he could maintain control demanded that when students did not behave or achieve at a desired level, a reason had to be found. With limited access to the bigger picture, it became easy for Barry to focus even more harshly on the student as an independent and responsible agent.

Adversality between the administration and teachers was a recurring theme. Barry consistently returned to the difference between the more collegial administration of the early years and the adversarial attitude and insecurity fostered by the current administration. Barry commented on communication between faculty:

> Part of the reason that we don't communicate with people is because it has been structured to make it ever more difficult to have communication. One of the major weaknesses in this school is communication. From top down, from bottom up, our weakest point is communication. We do not do it effectively.

Once again, the people of this school are locked in a self-perpetuating system of isolation and adversality. As Barry's experience suggests, the difference in relations between the administration and the faculty at different times has been due to a difference in culture and conversational type.

The final theme was Barry's insistence on a difference between the early years of the 1970s and the school climate of the late 1980s and 1990s. This is a theme that has been documented throughout this study; however, Barry's justifications for this interpretation point directly to the relational focus of his story. He constantly referred to a sense of ownership and community in the early years. In his conversation he repeatedly referred to respect; teachers were respected by other stakeholders in the early years, and now they are not. When asked what tools from the past could be used to create a better future, he responded by citing dialogue and respect. He stressed that a shared vision guided the actions of the early years, but now there are fragmented visions. Self-esteem emerged as another descriptor of the difference between the time periods. The gist of this point as made by Barry was that no one "gave a darn about the teacher's self-esteem"; everything is geared to making life better for the students. Dan and Steve agreed with this assessment and elaborated on it. All of these justifications are related to the limited number and quality of relationships available. Isolation breeds concern about one's own self-worth and about being respected by others.

Barry constructed a story of two time periods; an early period that was collegial, egalitarian, and relational; and a later one of isolation, irrelevancy, and failure. The moral of Barry's story is that to have a successful learning community, people need to develop collegial relationships facilitated by dialogic conversation, which, in turn, leads to a shared vision.

Sue's Story

Once again emotion guides us in understanding Sue's story of her experiences with educational change. Where Barry focused on interrelationships, Sue focused on intrapersonal aspects. The dominant theme of her story involved her professional self-esteem. Her early conversations in this study were characterized by a tentativeness and uncertainty about her professional efficacy that were uncharacteristic of her professional emotional state in years past. In the early years Sue was self-assured, in control, and decisive in her opinions—in other words, centered. What caused the change?

The balkanization and individualization of the school culture that resulting from the demise of the open classroom exacerbated Sue's tendency to isolate herself. She needed easy access to the other teachers, who provided the validation of her professional efficacy. With the open space gone, Sue became firmly entrenched in a self-contained classroom where her professional self-esteem eroded. Interpersonal interactions were less frequent and more difficult to create, and the opportunities provided by the administration were tightly controlled and contrived.

Because of Sue's high level of professional commitment, she took part in numerous change initiatives such as whole language learning, cooperative learning, effective teaching, and a state writing program. These opportunities provided her with more of a systemic view than other teachers had, but the input from the larger system was oriented solely to curriculum and instruction and also short-lived. Therefore, her exposure to critical issues was nonexistent, and her opportunity for interaction with others was temporary. The validation she received from these short-lived interactions was not enough to offset the deleterious effects of the pervasive isolation in her school.

A pivotal component in Sue's intrapersonal interpretations is conversation. Sue evidently thrives on dialogic conversation, as indicated by her eager participation in the conversational opportunity provided by this research. Also, her good feelings toward the open space of the early years support the idea that the conversational mode of that time was indeed dialogic. In the debriefing she wrote:

> As with all of the information that you passed on to us, they [the spiritual crisis and learning organization reading] explain a lot. The combination of the closed classroom plus the IPCs serve to "I-It" an environment in a hurry. Sometimes I wonder if all of us [the older group] are just suffering from post-partum depression because of our removal from the open space. It certainly was responsible for a great deal of the camaraderie we experienced. But again, one would think that

such a huge reformation would have been dealt with from an in-service point of view. Couldn't an administrator see what a drastic impact that would have on the lives of people who had just spent fifteen and twenty years in a completely different teaching environment?

Her service on the block scheduling committee must have afforded her an opportunity to fulfill her conversational needs, as indicated by the good feelings she conveyed about the accomplishments of that committee. However, she critically pointed out that when the schedule was implemented, the conversation ended:

> We don't talk about block scheduling at all. It is like we have it, so whatever. We just hope that it is working, but do we really know if it is? Our committee is working up a faculty survey, but as far as having a dialogue about something that is this important, something that is a huge change, there is nothing, no dialogue.

Conversation is important to Sue, but as she said, conversation with other professionals is critical because only other professionals can understand. In response to a question about whether this type of conversation should be part of our professional development experience, she replied,

> Absolutely, to keep us sane; involving professionals. Only other people who are "in the trenches" with us "get it." Shared experiences are everything, but we have reached the stage where our shared experiences are never given an opportunity to be shared, and that is unhealthy and stagnating.

Sue valued this type of conversation so much that she initiated the proposal to include it in the faculty in-service programs for our next school year. The importance that she attributes to this type of conversation undoubtedly relates to the change in estimation of her own professional worth that resulted from this research. In her debriefing she explains:

> Much of the way I feel about my career has been explained by providing me with theoretical references. The result of this is that my feeling of "aloneness," or isolation has abated. I realize that I, indeed, am not alone. There is a name and more importantly a reason for why I have been experiencing what I have been experiencing. By far, best of all, there is a solution. Therein lies the paradox. There is a solution, but will we ever get to the solution?

More than likely, dialogic conversation is the main ingredient of this solution. However, for Sue, theory also has a prominent place. In response to a debriefing question on the inclusion of theory in the feedback papers, Sue wrote as follows:

In reality, that is the very best time to interject theory. Theory devoid of an experience base is meaningless. I now understand why theory and philosophy are so difficult at the undergraduate level. They are not tied to experience or practice. Tied to experience and practice, a theoretical explanation crystallizes many occurrences. In our professional lives, "stuff" happens, and we often don't understand why. Theory gives us the why.

Sue is a person who thrives in a collegial environment, an interactive environment. To Sue, conversation is a vital ingredient in professional life. When the group conversation was held, Sue was not able to attend at first, because of another faculty committee meeting. After about an hour and a half, she arrived at our meeting and eagerly joined in the conversation. During that conversation, I noted a comment that explains her valuing of conversation and her changed opinion of her personal efficacy: ". . . my teaching has been enhanced . . . talking to other people . . . such a catharsis." In the open space, the boundaries between her class and the others were more permeable. Now her boundaries are rigid and tightly controlled by the structure, schedule, and culture of her school. Sue's message is that collegial conversation can offset the deleterious effects of this situation.

Dave's Story
Dave's story is best told in the context of these questions: Who is he? What does he need? What is he not getting from his school environment? Regarding the first question, Dave is a classroom teacher, a coach of two sports, a member of the Student Assistance Program, and a cooperating teacher for student teachers; but more deeply he is emotional, collegial, and spiritual. These qualities pervade his life and greatly enhance his effectiveness in dealing with problems and change in his personal life and in his extracurricular school work. While Dave is rewarded with success in his personal life and professional extracurricular activities because of his emotional, collegial, and spiritual focus, he is severely limited in the employment of these qualities in dealing with systemic problems and change in the non-extracurricular, teaching aspect of his professional life. Unfortunately, the hierarchical system and the balkanized and individualized culture of which he is a part fail to fully utilize these qualities, and this blunts his effectiveness in helping the system to deal with the systemic problems that it faces.

Ironically, the only aspects of his professional life that allow him the power and ownership that he experiences in his personal life are sports and his classroom. Dave is used to having control—a collegial and egalitarian contextualized control. In sports and at home, Dave, fully aware of the essential nature of a team, collegially negotiates with the other stakeholders. However, his lack of participation in the decisions controlling the main part of his professional life has created the same kind of territoriality and boundary control seen in the other participants.

Dave is fully aware of his limited power in relation to the systemic problems facing his profession and his school. Dave's interviews were dominated by his intense emotional response to his inability to participate more fully in dealing with these problems. His attitude toward his personal life and coaching is positive. But in regard to his position in the school system, he is suspicious, jaded, bitter, and to a degree paranoid concerning administrators and other change agents. The negative results of the interaction between the culture of isolation, the hegemonic hierarchy, and his own need to actualize himself are seen in his own words.

His focus on the administrators as the main perpetrators of the failure of educational change repeatedly surfaces:

> Dave: We have gone through a million different aspects of change. Overall, I would say that my impression of education in my twenty-eight years [as a teacher] is that the leadership doesn't have a clue. There is no leadership in the changes. We just bounce from one thing to another without any real research into it. Sometimes change comes from the top, it quickly falls apart, and then we go back to our old way. So the changes have been really superficial. Actually, they have been annoying. At times, they have left me more and more, I don't want to say bitter, but more skeptical about the leadership in our school district and in Pennsylvania education.
>
> Dave: I have adopted a philosophy of shut my door and do what is best from my experiences in education. Nobody checks on me, so I have come to the conclusion that nobody really gives a rat's ass about what I do in the end. So, pretty much, change happens for me by talking with fellow teachers, by going to conferences, and then sharing ideas and experimenting in my classroom. I think if teachers were given the opportunity, collectively we would change it for the better because we all want to do a better job. We all want to be professional. You want to help kids, so it is always up to my own personal motivation. It is always up to whatever I personally decide to do in my classroom. That is how change occurs. The motivation also comes from sharing ideas with people in my department, going to conferences, just experimenting, but not from the administration—it doesn't come from them.

One unfortunate result of the social structure and culture of Dave's environment is the creation of his belief that "I am alone and it is all up to me." An attitude like this leads to the belief that if other stakeholders (teachers, administrators, or students) are less efficient or effective than I am in fulfilling their responsibilities, then it is a personal failure on their part, not part of a systemic condition. Therefore, the reasoning continues: "So that I do not fail, it is imperative that I tightly monitor and control my room and my subsystem boundaries."

Dave's antipathy toward the administration, his unconscious awareness of balkanization in his stress on departmental action, and the need for teacher involvement in change continued to be evident in his commentary:

Dave: Change would have to come from the teacher, from the individual departments. Teachers can collectively meet with other teachers in their departments. Change has to come from the bottom up because the teachers, who will turn it into nothing, will dissipate anything from the top down. So any order from the top, like cooperative learning to outcome-based education, if I don't believe in the idea I will give superficial lip service and quickly kill the idea. I won't do it. It will look like I do, but if I don't believe in it I will find a way to trash it. If I believe in a change like the portfolio megaskills idea, I will find a way to do them in my classroom. So how change should happen is change should come from the departments, and then we turn it over to the top dogs for them to polish it, put it together, and package it. That's real change.

Dave: In the past, leadership has always been dictatorial. They feel that they have to be able to move the pieces, not let people do what they want to do, and not trust them. They are doing the "old style." They are doing exactly what the old-style teacher did. You know, where they would stand up and say, "Okay here is what you do, shut your mouth, pay attention, and just sit there and take it." So they are merely mimicking that style of leadership. There is very little room for us to change. Do I sound bitter?

Because of the nature of his school system and his experience, Dave limits his interpretations to either a top-down or bottom-up construct. His experience does not facilitate the development of a more collegial and collaborative view of education. The fact that he can share power and collaborate with others in his personal life and extracurricular activities but is denied this collegiality in his professional life fosters a sensitivity and aversion to bureaucratic centralized power. Dave exhibits a type of professional dissociation in that the way he deals with people and change in one part of his life (his teaching life) is different from the way he deals with change in the other parts (his home life and extracurricular professional life). This forced fragmentation results in the frustration and anxiety that he experiences.

Dave's need for collegial conversation was clear throughout the interviews. The link between his isolation and his need to talk was apparent in his answer to the question about whether dialogic conversation should be part of our professional development experience:

Dave: Definitely. I think that if a few years ago I had been involved in this kind of conversation, I would be more motivated to push for change—to share ideas. I would become more of a team player in breaking down the walls. However, right now like I told you before, I am alone in my room. Period. I'm happy at the moment when nobody bothers me because I do my own thing and leave at the end of the day. I am a little island. I know it is not healthy, but for my mental state and for my own growth, I do it. I do it to survive.

Ray: How about if time were actually built into the schedule for us to sit down and do this? Would you do it?

Dave: Yeah, I am sure that would be worthwhile. Collectively, we would come up with a lot of good ideas and ways to solve problems. But again I would have to be convinced that somebody would actually listen and help to work out and carry out our recommendations. We have done that in the past, but the ideas soon die out. So that is why I have backed off on all committees and groups. I don't get involved with any of that now because the effort doesn't pay off. But if I thought that these [ideas] would be implemented, yes, I would get involved. But I would not waste my time if we were only sitting around talking to feel good or to gripe; then I wouldn't bother.

An interesting difference between Dave and Sue is in their sense of their own efficacy. Sue's sense of professional efficacy was denigrated by her isolation. On the other hand, Dave has a pervasive sense that teachers could generate good ideas and solve problems, that the problem is with someone else—the personal failure of the administration or of other stakeholders. The difference in these attitudinal interpretations can be attributed to Dave's successful involvement and empowerment in activities that involve collective action. His efforts are validated on a daily basis in his home life, his sports activity, and his work with students in crisis. There is no doubt in his mind that he can do an effective job and that his intuitions are more accurate than those of outsiders (administration members, experts external to his system).

Earlier I alluded to Dave's pervasive spirituality. This driving force that energizes and focuses all other aspects of his life is disregarded by the school system in relation to the very thing that can benefit from it—educational change. It is spirituality that is denied by the objectification of Dave by the system and by his own objectification of other stakeholders. The deleterious effects of the hierarchical system and the culture of isolation nullify the virtues of an "I-Thou" relationship.

The result of all this is an enervating pessimism:

Dave: I like the idea of sharing information. I have no way to resolve problems, share information, or ask for help. There is no way to do that, and that fits into the realm of having power over my life; to help solve my professional problems. I keep saying that I only have control in my room—I have authority there. Beyond that I feel like I am totally helpless. So I care about the authority problem, sharing information, and just knowing that I am not alone. That is how I feel.
Ray: Any other final comments?
Dave: Yes. All the ideas [the ideas he encountered in this study] are great. Unfortunately, one more time it will come to nothing.
Ray: You turned into a skeptic.
Dave: Yes. It [this study] is nice work, but it will be put somewhere in a nice little closet and no one will give a rat's rear end about it. It will never affect our school. So nice paperwork, and I agree with it. I wish it could be done, but I think the walls are so high, and nobody gives a rat's rear end. It will never be injected into reality, which saddens me even more.
Ray: So you are a pessimist and a skeptic to the bitter end?
Dave: Yes, and I don't like to be and I hate myself for it because, like I said, in my own life I am the opposite. In my own family and everywhere else, I would never be this way. I'm never pessimistic, skeptical, or doubting. I always have hope and think that the best will happen. I always think that I can make an impact. I believe that in the other areas of my life. But here in my professional life what I had hoped to be a really positive experience turned into a shambles.

Who is Dave? Like the others, Dave is a caring, dedicated, effective professional, who over his entire career has striven to do the right thing. He is concerned to the point of becoming distraught, over the fact that his full potential as an educational professional has not been realized. He is aware that to realize this potential he needs to be empowered and to empower others; this can happen only in the egalitarian context of collegial collaboration.

Steve's Story

Steve's story is most interesting in his reflections on what he was like when he began his career, how he currently views his profession and himself, and how he arrived at his current state.

At the beginning of his career, Steve was idealistic, involved, collegially engaged with others, and innovative. He was involved in directing student theatrical productions, he was a cooperating teacher for student teachers, and he was an educational risk-taker. Now he sees himself as an isolated professional doing what he can in his own room, largely detached from his colleagues. Then and now, Steve is very precise and behaviorally controlling in the systematic pursuit of maintaining his classroom environment and achieving his educational goals. Also, Steve has a more systemic perspective than the other participants, who tended to focus on themselves or on the other stakeholders in the system. Steve's broader perspective includes an awareness of how the system functions and of the effects on the school system of the larger suprasystem described by him as "society."

Like the other participants, Steve is a member of a balkanized, individualized school culture that includes an adversarial relationship between administrators and teachers and excludes students from accessing power. Steve's reflections also indicate that the adversarial relationship extends to the students. An example of this will be given at the end of this story.

The story of Steve's early years, his current situation, and the intervening events is best told in his own words:

Steve: In the earlier part of my career there was that sense of the possible, and now I think it is more of a sense of resignation. Not in the sense that I'm going to resign but in the kind of resignation that this is how education is, and you are not going to change it. At first there was possibility, a time when you could see yourself as a change agent, and if reinforced by others, change would be possible. Somebody sitting alone moaning in his or her room isn't going to be effective until they start communicating. So any kind of change needs one to think that "I can do this," or think that it can happen. And suddenly when other people are saying the same thing and supporting each other, then you will have change. But as soon as you feel fragmented, isolated, or alienated, then the ideas begin to shut down. Then you begin to feel defensive, protective, and basically withdraw from the possibility that you have something to contribute. As you become isolated you become separated in the system from the others, and then you tend to just think that, well, I will just take care of myself. Cover your ass, cover yourself, go in your room and do your own thing—you know this kind of thing. So I think that you get pretty resigned to the idea that this is the way it is. You know it is true because you are physically in that little room, like Dilbert in his cubicle. That is the whole psychology of what is going on.

I asked Steve at what point in his career he felt like a change agent and at what point he felt fragmented and alienated. In his reply he discusses the social studies open classroom in relation to the larger system:

Steve: Well, the answer to the change agent part is when we as a department began to think that we could do what we wanted, and we did. We created and operated a whole new schedule. We had an autonomous kind of little school within a school. We were doing things, we had a program that wasn't anywhere else in the school. However, it needed to be more systemic. It needed to go throughout the whole system, but it was truncated. It became cut off, isolated, and then the whole program was broken up and kind of fragmented. It just withered away for lack of support. So I think that I felt most isolated and most unproductive when we knew we would have to go back to the old way of teaching. Going back was not moving in any direction, in this case it was stagnating. In a sense we were asked to deny everything that we had discovered up to that point. It was like, here is what we have discovered, we have piloted a program, and we have discovered some things. But they said that no it can't be right because we are just teachers; what you teachers found can't be true. Then we went backward. Any fool could see that. Not only were we asked to go backward, but then we were asked to maintain a status quo and stay there, which of course brings up one of the great ironies about a lot of the new change efforts involving block scheduling. We have been there. We were doing that a long time ago.

Ray: Do you feel fragmented and alienated right now?

Steve: I think so. I think that we pay a lot of lip service to change trends. I think that it is just the nature of the system.

Ray: So then the way we handle change is inevitable?

Steve: Yes, I think so. I mean it is inevitable because that is the way the system is structured to behave. I mean that school systems are pretty much geared to that sort of behavior. Every time I read about educational change or schools that try to change, they are basically no different than us. They try on certain things every now and then, like a block schedule, but they never really make any fundamental changes—unless they totally break off from the system. They form one of those magnet schools.

In an earlier conversation about the early years of the open school, Steve touched on collegiality, vision, and facilitation of professional conversation in the open classroom experience, and discussed change in educational systems generally:

Steve: I think that our open classroom experience was driven by the members of the department to meet the needs of education and the students at that particular time. We did this by observing, thinking about the problems, and then taking action. We tried things, we tinkered with them, reflected on them, and made adjustments. But the problem was that these needs and problems didn't only involve one department. Our problem was that you can't change a whole system by just changing one thing. The whole system doesn't run and can't be dictated to by one part of the system. In our case we had to try to deal with the whole school system.

In relation to issues of power and decision making during the open classroom period, Steve replied, "I tend to think that decisions were basically made by the department members, and not one individual. The group, despite all of the problems that that kind of decision making entails made it."

I asked if the vision as expressed by the department's philosophy of the 1970s was closely linked to the practice of the department:

> Steve: Yes, because we lived it. We lived the vision every day, and we used the constant feedback to solve the problems that came up. I'm just picturing in my mind what took place. Basically we would have to immediately solve the problems. We would get together and deal with them. We would kick them around and as a team go work on it some more. There was a constant team effort, and it was sort of like a science research and development team. We came up with ideas, worked on them, developed some procedures, and tried them out. We were constantly interacting with roadblocks and dealing with them. I think that one of the problems now that doesn't facilitate change is that the ability for teachers to relate to each other on a continual basis doesn't happen. This is a real handicap as far as making changes. Making change work happens when teachers are continually interrelating. It doesn't happen from the top down, or from outside the school from experts.
>
> Steve continued: There was a constant evolution of the vision. There was always another question, or an opportunity to raise a question. Don't get the impression that there was a point when we were done changing. There was always change. There always was an openness about changing the vision because it was always on-going.

Conversation is a key element in the difference between Steve's interpretation of himself as a change agent and as a fragmented and alienated individual:

> Steve: I am always amazed at how much can really be accomplished when teachers are allowed to talk to each other, or solve problems themselves. Given the time, if the system gives you the time, I think we can accomplish great things. Unfortunately the system that is created at most educational institutions does not facilitate that sort of thing. If you look at the time that teachers spend talking to each other, and how the day is structured, it doesn't facilitate this kind of interaction. There is a lack of flexibility that allows teachers to do that. There seems to be this notion that conversation among teachers has to be built into formal department meetings that happen at an exact time, not on an on-going basis. Now you can't have a conversation with other people in your department about an issue because the system has become inflexible. We had created a situation where communication was very flexible, and that has slowly eroded over the years.

After introducing Steve to Buber's ideas on relationships, I asked him if any of these ideas related to the early years of the social studies department:

Steve: I would tend to say that earlier it was more I-Thou than I-It because we were together in the sense that we had more of an open working relationship. We had to depend on each other and communicate with each other. We had to solve problems together more often, so we had to overcome our own individual inadequacies and help each other.

Steve is academically and idealistically oriented, providing another context in which to analyze change during his career:

Steve: We are an institution that deals with ideas and yet when you look at how often we deal with ideas, it is amazing. I would be interested in actually studying how much of a teacher's time is actually concerned with behavior that was of a reflective nature—that deals with ideas. Maybe I am just an anomaly, but I think that these kinds of conversations are about ideas, and people don't talk about ideas. We are supposed to be an institution, an agent of society that is responsible for how ideas are passed on in our culture. Therefore, if we are responsible for the intellectual development of the youth of our society, then I think it is imperative that we have an opportunity to talk about ideas and to share them. I remember hearing a keynote speaker at a workshop who said that we should have time in our day for professional reading and reflection. You should be able to go somewhere and sit there for an hour and just read an article about your profession—read the things and talk about them. But it never happens, and I always wonder why that never happens. I guess it is because we are becoming less concerned with intellectual development and ideas and more concerned with custodial care.

Ray: Dave might also say that this is the case because teachers playing with ideas through collegial conversation threaten the administration. Administrators might be concerned that the faculty will come up with ideas that don't fit into their plan. What do you think of that?

Steve: I agree with that because it happened in the past. I mean that we came up with ideas, didn't we? Then they had a crisis on their hands, and they had to do something about it . . . I think that at our school education tends to be reactive, tends to be something that is done because it is a trend, because it is perceived as something that ought to happen. There is very little in the way of a philosophical foundation or root that comes from the grassroots experience of the people. So there is a lack of trust in our ability to execute change, to be creative enough to do it on our own. This creates the idea that it has to come from the outside, that it has to be validated by some sort of external force, because we don't have the ability or are not smart enough to bring about the change ourselves. This leads to the fact that changes are sort of tried on. We will try this and see how it works. There is never a real understanding about why we are changing. Things always seem to be done in a very superficial way, ending with the change happening on paper only. There is a lot of talk and a lot of paper, so you have this enormous record of a lot of talk about change—a lot of description and jargon. Verbal description rather than the actual behavior of the individuals drives a lot of change, so nobody ever takes a hard look at what actually happens. Something is promoted as a change if it can be described well, if current jargon can be used, and if it can be employed somewhere in the system. That is the way change happens.

I mentioned the large number of committees both in the early years and in the recent restructuring years, and I asked Steve if there was a difference in teachers' perception of their involvement during these two periods:

Steve: There was a desire on my part in the 1970s to be involved because I felt a sense of ownership and a sense of desire on my own part to be part of those changes. I was convinced that something ought to be done. I was introduced to ideas, and then I was allowed to develop those ideas as they would apply to our situations. That was the critical difference between the way it happened in the 1970s and now. We were introduced to the ideas and then allowed to run with them. Now with block scheduling and portfolios, they were something that needed to be inserted as opposed to developing an idea and implementing it. We were told that block scheduling was a way to deal with the school day. Well, why do we need to deal with the school day? If block scheduling is the answer, what are the questions? I think asking questions seems to be the difference between the way I perceive it now and the way I thought it was back then. Now, asking questions seems to be perceived [by the administration] as a threat. When teachers start asking too many questions, the leaders go into some sort of defensive mode. There is a general fear of questions, so we [the teachers] in a sense are being denied what we naturally would do.

At one point I asked Steve if he was satisfied with the results of change from the beginning of his career to the end:

Steve: No, I am not satisfied the way it [change] ended up because I think that it has come full circle. We have lost opportunities. When I say full circle, I mean it is back to the status quo. The changes have evaporated mostly because you are dealing with fundamental social institutions, and with them it is more difficult to make changes stick even if they are found to be valuable. I think that individuals change because they make the adjustments that are necessary for themselves professionally. Maybe that is why they become frustrated, because they feel the system is never going to change.

Ray: What do you miss from those early years? Is there anything that you would want to recapture?

Steve: Camaraderie is something that is often talked about among teachers that are my age, that is something that is missing. Also, I would want to recapture the perception that we are going somewhere, that we are going forward, that we are achieving and growing. I think there was a point at which maybe, metaphorically, as soon as the walls went up, growth was stunted. I felt that we were in a continuous retreat and I coped with it, but it was never as exciting as the time when we were continuing to move; dealing with new problems, always growing, and always developing something that was on the horizon. Now it is just stonewalling; it is just cover your ass and protect your own interest. There is a lack of selfless motivation about it; now it is more of a selfish motivation. So that is what I think I have missed [the perception that we are going somewhere] for about twenty years or so. Now it is a matter of how can we create the illusion of movement.

Steve told me about a problem that he had with a student during the study period at the end of the day. After telling the story, he said that such game-playing (over the use of the lavatory) pretty well sums up the whole story of coming full circle at our school. He was correct in his interpretation in the context of his current professional situation; however, what he encountered can also be used to provide a broader interpretation of educational change.

In our school at the end of every day we have a "flex" period in which students are assigned to a teacher for study purposes. The real need for a flex period is to provide meeting time for the band and the chorus and to accommodate the student athletes who must leave early for a game. Without the flex period, the band and chorus would not be able to meet during the school day, and the athletes would miss part of their last class. Despite numerous recommendations by other schools who were using a block schedule, to cancel the flex period, the political strength of the band boosters forced the administration to provide a space for band and chorus practice within the block schedule. Coming at the end of the day, the flex period creates a difficult situation for both teachers and students. Teachers are required to maintain a quiet study environment, while most students are burned out from the long school day and want to socialize. A selling point for the block schedule was that vandalism would drop. To facilitate this outcome, the administration ordered that no students would be allowed to go to the lavatory during the flex period, to prevent lavatory and hall vandalism.

Steve's lavatory story is one that all the teachers could tell. A student asks Steve to go to the lavatory. Of course, he says no, which leads to resistance from the student, who, after vociferously arguing her point, finally returns to her seat. The results of this exchange are that everyone is now off task, Steve is angry, the student is angry and resentful toward Steve, and the relationship between them is damaged. On a deeper level, Steve's need for control is validated, and so is the child's act of resistance to this perceived injustice.

Earlier in the debriefing conversation, Steve alluded to this situation in a way that is indicative of his need for classroom control and of his feelings about students during the flex period:

> I thought that I could read today during the, quote, study club [implying that very little if any studying actually takes place during this time]. I thought that I would be able to sit on those people as I usually do, and since they are conditioned not to say a word until 2:30 I would be able to think about this [my feedback papers]. I couldn't get one thought because right away, as soon as I sat down, some ninth-grader wanted to go to the bathroom, and I had to deal with that whole issue.

Steve's interpretation is that education has deteriorated to surreal game-playing over a student's need to go to a lavatory. His interpretation that there is a lack of responsibility on the part of the students, in this case revealed by the girl's resistance to the lavatory rule, once again reductionistically focuses Steve on only one aspect of a complex situation. Situations like this facilitate the development of narrow, modernistic teacher interpretations that block the development of a systemic view and block the belief that other stakeholders (in this case the students) should be empowered.

On a deeper level, this incident reveals how the hegemonic hierarchical structure and culture of isolation of this school results in Steve's need to control the classroom environment, in the alienation and objectification of the stakeholders, and in both types of stakeholders (teacher and student) focusing adversarially on each other instead of on collaborating and learning. This hierarchical situation becomes a power game that results in the stakeholders becoming adversaries instead of partners; for the teacher, the result is a focus on standards and student responsibility instead of on ideas and on collegiality with the other stakeholders.

Steve's interpretations and experiences show that educators must first deal with the critical issues of the use and distribution of power, the nature of relationships within the school, and the type of conversation that occurs, instead of with secondary and mechanical aspects of the system such as the curriculum and instruction. In this school, the primary critical issues have been resolved by returning to a traditional modernistic system with paper illusions of movement. The result for Steve is a career shift from change agent to custodian.

Dan's Story

Dan's story is unique in its focus, in that his primary concern is curriculum and instruction. As our conversation unfolded, the themes that recurred in the other participants' stories did not surface in Dan's. Therefore in our last conversation I asked him to tell the story of educational change during his career:

> Dan: Probably the main change would deal with the direction that we were given [by the administration]. Starting with my first years, which would have been the 1960s, direction would have consisted of handing teachers a textbook, and saying this is the book that you will be working from. No lesson plans, no mission statement, no goals, no outcomes, no standards. Then we moved into the building that we presently occupy, and the biggest change was the initiative undertaken by social studies and English with the modular scheduling and everything else. I think that the most significant changes in curriculum began at that time because we freed ourselves from the traditional lock-step pattern that the students followed. Then in a few years after that, in English we became aware that there were too many possibilities available for students, and we added a traditional option in which we went from quarterly courses to semester courses to full-year courses. However, as the school got larger, scheduling problems increased, so we really went full cycle and came back to more traditional and tracked lock-step courses again. That would take us to the early 1980s, at which time we started breaking out of that area again and offering options to the students. Today only the ninth and tenth grades are still traditional; eleventh and twelfth grade are semester-length electives, as well as nine-week electives.
>
> Ray: As I listened, I realized that your entire story was about curriculum and instruction. Other people talked about isolation and power, but your focus seems to be on your teaching. Is this a correct assessment of your work?
>
> Dan: Yes, it would be correct. I think that the way the building is currently designed does promote more isolation, but for me I don't mind that. I feel that I am more curriculum oriented than I was earlier. Before, I did plays, journalism, sold tickets at games, helped out at track meets. It seemed like I had a lot of free time, where now I am definitely much more focused on curriculum and spending the time during the day getting things done. You also have to keep in mind that I don't have a cross section of students, I have top-level students; and I don't do well with lower-level students. Thank you, Barry, for being willing to take those classes.
>
> Ray: Some teachers feel their empowerment or lack of power is important to them. I would make a guess that you always have felt empowered when you go into your classroom (in terms of) curriculum, instruction, and classroom management. Do you have all of the power that you need or want?

Dan: That is correct, because maybe I don't want as much as some people have. But I like the way you said it—I have all the power that I need or want. I never really felt that I was inhibited in doing what I really wanted to do in class. I honestly don't know of any time in the whole thirty-nine years that I was told you must teach this. I do think for me, and we are back on curriculum again, that the best curriculum guides were the ones that we had before the planned courses we have now.

At this point, I moved the conversation to emotions, to see how Dan would connect his concern about curriculum and instruction with emotion:

Dan: I think that the times that I get most emotional are when the district raises class size. You receive praise for what you are doing, but you are given situations where you can't do justice to what you have received praise for. And some of the times, that is tied to the times when class size is large. I think if students are to be given more choices, you can't have higher [numbers in] classes. You are depriving students of doing things because the numbers are higher, and they don't get the exposure because the downtime is too great for each student. This is something that bothers me.

Ray: What is interesting is that once again you are focused on curriculum and instruction, and you are getting emotional about that. Other people get emotional about things that happen to them personally, but I guess that you focus on curriculum and instruction because curriculum and instruction is a personal thing for you.

Dan: It is personal. I didn't really think about it that way before, but you are right, it is personal for me.

Ray: It seems to me that the spiritual component in your professional life is the relationship that you have with your teaching, which could be defined as your curriculum and instruction. This is what kept you centered all of these years.

Dan: It did, you are right. I never really thought about it that way, but you are right.

A question on spirituality, in the context of the Buber material, brought to light another aspect of Dan's story:

Dan: Spirituality has become more meaningful to me over the years. But as I see the whole concept of my religious growth, I think that I have a tendency to apply that to all phases of my life. I feel much more driven toward excellence than what I once did. I want to return [something] in kind to the classes that I teach. In other words, if I am expecting excellence from them, then I must also do it. This whole computer thing is another factor that has driven me, and the students who want to do well in my classes know they must drive toward excellence. I do feel that in

	education how you present yourself is also important It is not just what you present but how we as teachers present ourselves to our students. So that would be my I-Thou relationship with my students.
Ray:	So you see continuity between your personal religious growth and your instructional habits here at school?
Dan:	I think as I started teaching it was what I can do for the students. Now it is more of what I can enable the students to do for themselves. It is that empowerment thing. The downside of that is if I had a cross section of all kinds of students I would be a very frustrated person because the few poor students that I have to deal with who are not doing well, respond to a well-placed phone call to a parent.
Ray:	At this point in your career, is everything else superfluous if it doesn't deal with curriculum and instruction?
Dan:	Yes.
Ray:	Any final comments?
Dan:	I was interested in seeing what the others have said, because I realize now that my perception is different from how the others see things. I like having my own space and dealing with my own space the way I want to deal with it.
Ray:	So you wouldn't see the open space as a panacea?
Dan:	No, but I liked having the open space because I learned from other teachers in observing what they were doing. One other thing is that there were workshops that I thought were worthwhile, and I felt that they impacted on me in promoting changes.

Dan has avoided many of the problems generated by the hierarchical bureaucracy and culture of isolation in which he exists, through his evolving spirituality and his focus on his pedagogy. In addition, the type of students (motivated, upper-level students) that he teaches are less likely to trigger the postmodern problems experienced by the other participants. These adaptations in his professional life have acted as buffers against the changes and manipulations that have swirled around him. As long as he has control of his classroom, his pedagogy, and the type of students he teaches, he will be insulated from the vagaries of the system as experienced by the other participants. The balkanization and individualization of the school culture has seemingly worked to his advantage. However, in the broader context of the whole school environment, Dan's adaptation to these cultural forms helps to perpetuate the inegalitarian and oppressive nature of the school.

The Story of Educational Change

Inevitably, the study of a complex situation produces as many new questions as it provides answers. This research proved to be no different.

Through the use of post-formal professional development strategies, can teachers develop the skills needed to deal with the issues of power that deny their inclusion in policy making, develop a systemic view of their profession that informs their practice, and gain the knowledge that facilitates a critical construction of their practice? The answer is "maybe."

On one hand, the evidence suggests that post-formal professional development strategies have the potential to facilitate an understanding of change and the empowerment of teachers. However, this research has also identified a serious impediment to the post-formal development of educators: the systemic imperviability to change that is both insidious and pervasive.

Systemic Imperviability to Authentic Educational Change

Why was this educational system able to so assiduously resist the efforts of these career teachers? In the later years, one could argue, the hierarchical and cultural aspects of their school, reinforced by their tacit acceptance of isolation and disempowerment, presented an insurmountable barrier of modernistic isolation and balkanization that would be nearly impossible to remove. Also, in retrospect, the demise of the open classroom could be attributed to the change in administration, their teachers' lack of technical pedagogical knowledge, the lack of systemic knowledge, their incapacity to acquire a critical perspective (especially in the context of stakeholder inclusion), and their inability to sustain community and to foster the spirituality that was manifest in that community.

On a broader scale, Gary Anderson (1998) deconstructed participatory reform in education and found much of it to be "bogus, superficial, or ineffective" (p. 571). His analysis revealed how participation actually becomes a form of public relations exercise, designed to protect an institution's current practice; how participation mechanisms can become technologies of control; and how structures that are supposed to enhance participation often become sites of collusion between groups of stakeholders against others (Anderson, 1998). The systemic imperviability to change fostered by these outcomes of bogus participatory change are endemic not only to the institutions studied by Anderson but also to the school of the participants in this study.

However, another locus of imperviability lies specifically in the attitude of the participants. Banathy (1996b) discusses people's and systems' reactions to change by identifying four possible orientations toward change. Of the four, two seem to fit the participants in this study. A "reactive orientation" is one where "we are dissatisfied with the present, long for the past, and want to return to what was. We attempt to unmake changes and romanticize about the good old days when life was simple. We drive toward the future by looking in the rearview mirror and focusing on where we have been instead of where we want to go" (Banathy, 1996b, p. 38).

This matches the participants' insistence on the need to establish standards (like those we had in the old days), on promoting student responsibility for their actions (in the old days students were more responsible), and on expelling those who resist (a common practice in the old days). The angst and perturbation, the reflective questioning, and the drive to initiate positive change that accompanied the adaptation to the open classroom is not what is seen in the rearview mirror. What are viewed, instead, are the standards, student responsibility, and draconian measures of control that were characteristic of the period before the open space. These characteristics are simply more applicable to the current traditional, regressive educational environment. The conversation and communality of the open-classroom era only appeared in the rearview mirror when elicited by this post-formal conversation. If the reflective questioning and the spiritually driven motivation to create something new and better are not present, then post-formal conversation and communality are indeed irrelevant.

Banathy's "inactive orientation" is also relevant. "The label 'inactive'. . . is misleading. A great deal of energy and effort is spent on preventing change. The operating principle is preserving stability at all cost, and it takes a lot of work to keep things from changing. The inactivist says things may not be the best today, but they are good enough, or as good as can be expected. If nothing is done, things will stay as they are, and that is what we want" (Banathy, 1996b, p. 39). All the participants, including myself, unceasingly patrol the boundaries of our territory and assiduously maintain control in our classrooms. Newness of any kind is a threat to the security of our sameness. The prize for our diligence is a steady state of predictable security. Therefore, resistance to change is not futile but career enhancing. How else can one survive?

Banathy's other orientations, "preactivist" and "interactive," are both characterized by an acceptance of, if not an invitation to, the opportunity that change provides. These orientations are in the post-formal realm in that the interactivist places the past, present, and future in an interactive relationship, and the preactivist prepares for change and exploits its opportunities (Banathy, 1996b). Therefore, the current status of the participants is a mixture of the first two orientations, while any elements of the other two appear to be long gone.

Another reason why this human system is able to so effectively resist change is that alienation permeates the whole system. In this system, all the stakeholders are alienated from each other, and to make matters worse, this alienation has a special ability to resist any attempts to build community or change the system. Warren Breed (1971) talks about alienation as resentment and inauthenticity, both of which are evident in this system. "Alienation is not only a subjective feeling of resentment but also an expression of the objective conditions which expose a person to forces beyond his understanding and control" (Breed, 1971, p. 198). All the stakeholder resentment that arises from a condition of alienation is intensified by the duplicitous inauthenticity of the other stakeholders. "A relationship, institution, or society is inauthentic if it provides the appearance of responsiveness while the underlying condition is alienating" (Breed, 1971, p. 199). The disparity between the appearance of empowerment and the realities of teacher involvement, in a committee system tightly controlled by the administration, diminishes the teachers' professional esteem and creates an adversarial relationship with the administration. The disparity between the appearance of empowerment and the realities of student empowerment by the classroom teacher result in the same diminished self-esteem and adversarial relationships, this time between teacher and student. Administrators often decry the teachers' refusal to take action when "empowered" by the administrators. "To be alienated is to experience a sense of not belonging, and to feel that one's efforts are without meaning. To be involved inauthentically is to feel cheated and manipulated" (Breed, 1971, p. 199). The virulence that often characterizes the interactions between stakeholders is the direct effect of this alienating inauthenticity.

These partial explanations of the imperviability of our school system have one thing in common—they are interactive in requiring a similar response from the other stakeholders. Reactive and inactive orientations are not indicative of one part of a system but characteristic of the whole system. The inauthentic alienation reported by Breed is also systemic in its manifestation. In other words, structures or actions that facilitate imperviability to change are *systemic;* they are not isolated occurrences in one or two parts of the system. In order to be thoroughly understood, imperviability requires a holistic view. Therefore, if a teacher is to properly understand the actions of an administrator or student, the teacher must develop the skill to see the multidimensional aspect or the positioning of the administration or the student within the larger systemic environment.

The Potential of Post-Formal Professional Development

I now believe that the potential of post-formal professional development to affect educational change is conditional upon the holistic application of many post-formal techniques. The effectiveness of post-formalism is directly related to the synergetic effect created by the interaction of the individual post-formal elements, including post-formal conversation, the psychoanalytical analysis of place, autobiographical reflection, the analysis of the social construction of meaning, the development of a critical contextualization of one's experience, and the development of a systemic view.

Activating the potential of post-formal professional development requires the inclusion of young and old teachers, the development of a risktaker attitude concerning the inclusion of other stakeholders (students, and parents) in the conversation, and a commitment to community building through post-formal conversation. Other requirements are the acquisition and critical construction of skills and knowledge like systems thinking, critical awareness, critical autobiographical reflection on place and time, examination of the construction of individual and collective meanings, and recognition and integration of affect. There must be a commitment to external professional development of a critical nature so that critical knowledge and skills can inform the community's indigenous knowledge. Finally, there must be a realization that post-formal activity may be construed as a subversive activity and should be pursued as such. Spaces need to be actively appropriated for conversation, and the structures of the system (the union, the committee structure, the larger community, and even the administration) need to be infiltrated. Most importantly, when opportunities present themselves, the stakeholders must be able and willing to act.

A principal lesson from this research is that veteran teachers want to converse and will give time to engage in this kind of activity. They will incorporate educational theory into their conversation and construction of meaning if it is introduced in an authentic context.

What Did I Learn?

Change cannot be accomplished by individuals or by small groups, either from the top down or from the bottom up. In the early years of this story, the assistant superintendent, who in Bertalanffy's terminology was a "leading part," established a coalition and set in motion a change initiative that would affect the school for more than fifteen years. However, this too did pass. In more recent years, teachers, as individuals and in small groups, initiated changes that were quickly assimilated by the system. I have learned from this study that the potential for significant change can come only from the development of a community that is spiritually bound together by a shared vision.

I am concerned by the potential effect of the loss of these career teachers on the ability of the other members of the system to build a sustainable community. As our group nears retirement age, our valuable experiential knowledge will be lost and will not inform those who are younger. A characteristic of modernistic education is the lack of cultural transmission of experience from one generation of teachers to another. The experience of the older teachers is actually cultural knowledge of their place over time, and it is lost because of the lack of post-formal conversation. Furthermore, can a community be sustained without a communicated history? The lack of temporal and experiential perspective promotes the school as a way station, not as a community.

Patterns

To further explore what I had learned, I framed my research questions in the context of Bohm and Peat's concepts of explicate and implicate order (Bohm and Peat, 1987; Peat, 1991). Bohm and Peat see hidden patterns of order, some of which are deeper and more hidden than others. The first level of order is called explicate order. This order of reality is relatively discerned due to the simple patterns and invariants that repeat themselves in similar and easily recognizable ways. The explicate order appears to be a pattern of simple cause and effect linearity (Kincheloe and Steinberg, 1996), which seemingly lends itself to easy explanation.

On the other hand, the implicate order is one of nonlinear holism involving a much deeper structure of reality. On this level, "ostensible separateness vanishes and all things seem to become a part of a larger unified structure" (Kincheloe and Steinberg, 1996, p. 179). Whereas the explicate level allows the more formalistic categorization and generalization of reality, the implicate level is too complex for formal processes to discern the deeper meanings. The implicate order is a process whereby the order of reality becomes an enfolded structure that is not easily detected by empirical methods of inquiry. In an educational context, the explicate order is the primary focus of attention, with schools rarely penetrating to the greater, more holistic complexity of the implicate level that orders their reality.

In the context of *Teacher Talk*, the explicate order was manifested by the participants in terms of standards, individual responsibility, classroom control, and the separation of young and old teachers. The implicate order was explored through the application of systems theory, critical theory, affect control theory, conversation, and spirituality. The implicate order was glimpsed in the participants' interpretations concerning teacher culture, the centralized and hierarchical context of power, the importance of collegial vision and community, and the importance of conversation.

In relation to Bohm's context of order and to our participation in this study, I ask the question: Where were the participants and I in our understanding of our reality from the beginning of the research to the end? In relation to the participants, I would surmise that, at the beginning of this research, their interpretations of reality were affected not only by their interactions with the other stakeholders in their school system but also by an abstract explicative phenomenon that pervades all of education and is reinforced by external sources such as media, textbook publishers, and outside experts. Initially the participants' sole awareness and unconditional acceptance of the explicate negated their possibility of realizing the implicate. In other words, their reality was solely attached to the superficiality of the explicate order. I believe that through their research experience they have a burgeoning awareness of the implicate order.

As for myself, I started this research with a praxis orientation of the explicate and the implicate. Now I have an awareness of the even greater complexity of the relationships between the components of the implicate order of education. My awareness has been broadened by the compelling humanism, empathy, and caring that is inherent in a post-formal exploration of the implicate order of human experience. I also learned that doing this kind of post-formal qualitative research provides an opportunity for the researcher to become a transformative intellectual (Giroux, 1993) and to create opportunities that may lead to the transformation of others. Finally, going into this research, I would characterize my professional activity as driven by a concern for social justice. What was added during the research was an equally important paradigm of caring. My experience in this research encouraged the feminist theories of caring, of which I was intellectually aware, to become fully integrated into my visceral interpretation and interaction with the meanings constructed by others. In a sense, I moved from a Kohlbergian justice paradigm (Kohlberg, 1981) to a synthesis including the caring paradigm explicated by Carol Gilligan (1982; Gilligan et al., 1988) and Nel Noddings (1992). Most important, the caring component of this synthesis is the element that *morally* grounds post-formal inquiry as a professional development method. This is the safeguard against a nihilistic relativism. Similarly, even though I was intellectually aware of the role of spirituality in fostering motivation and commitment to a vision, at the beginning of this research, spirituality had a low level of priority for me. However, as spirituality emerged in the conversation, I realized that it was a powerful and integral component in educational change. I also realized the relationship of spirituality to a commitment to justice and caring.

Applications

Having experienced post-formal inquiry as a professional development method, I believe that there are groups of people in an educational system who can benefit from this type of inquiry. Experienced and beginning teachers can achieve empowering and egalitarian community. Pre-service teachers can develop support networks as students and make a better transition to the profession. Administrators are provided with an opportunity to safely discuss alternatives to modernistic system approaches with other educators.

Perhaps you have noticed that students are not included as a target group. Ideally, they and other stakeholders (parents and other community members) must be included. I wholeheartedly agree with their inclusion. However, I also argue that the positions of the participants in this study concerning student empowerment are typical of the feelings of most educators. My proposition is that if the teachers and administrators can become part of an egalitarian community, then they will be secure enough to see the ideal and practical necessity of including and empowering all other stakeholders. My pragmatic approach should in no way suggest that post-formal inquiry is not appropriate for these other stakeholders.

I leave my study of educational change with important questions and concerns about the future of free public education and its ability to survive the transition from the modern to the postmodern. After thirty years of failed change, I wonder if, indeed, the situation is hopeless. The answer to that question will be written in concert by all of the stakeholders in the American educational system.

References

Ackoff, R. L. (1981). *Creating the corporate future.* New York: John Wiley & Sons.

Alter, J. (1996, April 8). Busting the big blob. *Newsweek,* 40.

Anderson, G. L. (1989). Critical ethnography in education: Origins, current status, and new directions. *Review of Educational Research, 59* (3), 249–270.

Anderson, G. L. (1998). Toward authentic participation: Deconstructing the discourses of participatory reforms in education. *American Educational Research Journal, 35* (4), 571–603.

Apple, M. (1986). *Teachers and texts: A political economy of class and gender relations in education.* Boston: Routledge & Kegan Paul.

Association of American Geographers. (1970). *The high school geography project: Geography in an urban age.* London: Macmillan.

Avers, D., Broadbent, M., Ferguson, T., Gabriele, S., Lawson, T., McCormick, S., & Wotruba, D. (1996). Design conversation and systems design: Group report. *Proceedings of the Eighth International Conversation on Comprehensive Design of Social Systems, Pacific Grove, California,* 1–42.

Banathy, B. H. (1992). *A systems view of education: Concepts and principles for effective practice.* Englewood Cliffs, NJ: Educational Technology Publications.

Banathy, B. H. (1996a). Conversation as social systems design. *Educational Technology, 36* (1), 39–41.

References

Banathy, B. H. (1996b). *Designing social systems in a changing world.* New York: Plenum Press.

Benking, H. (1997). *Sharing Spaces.* [On-line]. Available at http://newciv.org.cob/members/SharingSpaces.htm.

Bennett, K. P., & LeCompte, M. D. (1990). *The way schools work: A sociological analysis of education.* New York: Longman.

Bertalanffy, L. Von. (1968). *General systems theory.* New York: Braziller.

Bohm, D. (1990). *On dialogue.* Ojai, CA: David Bohm Seminars.

Bohm, D. (1992). *Thought as a system.* New York: Routledge.

Bohm, D., & Peat, F. (1987). *Science, order, and creativity.* New York: Bantam Books.

Branson, R. K. (1987). Why the schools can't improve: The upper limit hypothesis. *Journal of Instructional Development, 10* (4), 15–26.

Breed, W. (1971). *The self-guiding society.* New York: Free Press.

Buber, M. (1988). *Eclipse of God.* Atlantic Highlands, NJ: Humanities Press International.

Buber, M. (1992). *On intersubjectivity and cultural creativity.* Chicago: University of Chicago Press.

Butchart, R. E. (1998). Introduction. In R. E. Butchart & B. McEwan, (Eds.), *Classroom discipline in American schools* (pp. 1–18). Albany, NY: State University of New York Press.

Butchart, R. E., & McEwan, B. (eds.). (1998). *Classroom discipline in American schools.* Albany, NY: State University of New York Press.

Canady, R. L. (1995). *Block scheduling: A catalyst for change in high school.* Princeton, NJ: Eye on Education.

Carr, A. A. (1997). Conversation at Pennsylvania State University.

Checkland, P. (1981). *Systems thinking, systems practice.* New York: John Wiley & Sons.

Checkland, P., & Scholes, J. (1990). *Soft systems methodology.* New York: John Wiley & Sons.

Clandinin, D. J., & Connelly, F. M. (1995). *Teachers' professional knowledge landscapes.* New York: Teachers College Press.

Cocalico School District. (1969). *Long range development plan.* Denver, PA: Cocalico School District.

Cocalico School District. (1970). *Cocalico School District administrative review and recommendations 1969/70, curriculum committee reports, September 1970.* Denver, PA: Cocalico School District.

Collen, A. (1996). Reflection and metaphor in conversation. *Educational Technology, 36* (1), 54–55.

Connelly, F., & Clandinin, D. J. (eds.). (1988). *Teachers as curriculum planners: Narratives of experience.* New York: Teachers College Press.

Connelly, F., & Clandinin, D. J. (eds.). (1999). *Shaping a professional identity: Stories of educational practice.* New York: Teachers College Press.

Cuban, L. (1993). *How teachers taught: Constancy and change in American classrooms, 1890–1980.* New York: Teachers College Press.

Dolbec, A. (1996). The gestalt approach as a relevant framework to facilitate the design process. *Educational Technology, 36* (1), 17–19.

Doll, Jr., W. (1993). *A post-modern perspective on curriculum.* New York: Teachers College Press.

Elkind, D. (1995). School and family in the postmodern world. *Phi Delta Kappan, 77* (1), 8–14.

Ellsworth, E. (1989). Why doesn't this feel empowering? Working through the repressive myths of critical pedagogy. *Harvard Educational Review, 59* (3), 297–324.

Faules, D. F., & Alexander, D. C. (1978). *Communication and social behavior: A symbolic interaction perspective.* Menlo Park, CA: Addison-Wesley.

Fessler, R. (1995). Dynamics of teacher career stages. In T. R. Guskey & M. Huberman (Eds.), *Professional development in education: New paradigms and practices* (pp. 171–192). New York: Teachers College Press.

Fontana, A., & Frey, J. H. (1994). Interviewing: The art of science. In N. K. Denzin & Y. S. Lincoln (Eds.), *Handbook of qualitative research* (pp. 361–376). Thousand Oaks, CA: Sage Publications.

Freire, P., & Macedo, D. P. (1996). A dialogue: Culture, language and race. In P. Leistyna, A. Woodrum, & S. A. Sherblom (Eds.), *Breaking free: The transformative power of critical pedagogy* (pp. 199–228). Cambridge, MA: Harvard Educational Review.

Gilligan, C. (1982). *In a different voice.* Cambridge, MA: Harvard University Press.

Gilligan, C., Ward, J. V., Taylor, J. M., & Bardige, B. (1988). *Mapping the moral domain.* Cambridge, MA: Harvard University Press.

Giroux, H. (1988). *Teachers as intellectuals: Toward a critical pedagogy of learning.* Westport, CT: Bergin & Garvey.

Giroux, H. (1993). Teachers as transformative intellectuals. In H. S. Shapiro & D. E. Purpel (Eds.), *Critical social issues in American education* (pp. 273–277). New York: Longman.

Giroux, H. (1994). *Disturbing pleasures: Learning about popular culture.* New York: Routledge.

Greene, J. C. (1994). Qualitative program evaluation: Practice and promise. In N. K. Denzin & Y. S. Lincoln (Eds.), *Handbook of qualitative research* (pp. 530–544). Thousand Oaks, CA: Sage Publications.

Gribbin, J. (1995). *Schrödinger's kittens and the search for reality.* New York: Little, Brown.

Guba, E. G., & Lincoln, Y. S. (1989). *Fourth generation evaluation.* Newbury Park, CA: Sage.

Guskey, T. R., & Huberman, M. (1995). *Professional development in education: New paradigms and practices.* New York: Teachers College Press.

Habermas, J. (1995). *Moral consciousness and communicative action.* Cambridge, MA: MIT Press.

Hargreaves, A. (1994). *Changing teachers, changing times.* New York: Teachers College Press.

Holly, P. (1991). Action research: The missing link in the creation of schools as centers of inquiry. In A. Lieberman & L. Miller (Eds.), *Staff development for education in the 90's* (2nd Ed., pp. 133–157). New York: Teachers College Press.

Horn, R. A. (1995 Winter). Teacher background, beliefs and training as critical variables in the implementation of outcome-based education. *Pennsylvania Journal of Teacher Leadership,* 30-34.

Horn, R. A. (1999a). The dissociative nature of educational change. In J. L. Kincheloe (Ed.), *The post-formal reader: Cognition and education.* New York: Garland.

Horn, R. A. (1999b). Joe L. Kincheloe: Teacher-as-researcher. *Educational Researcher, 28* (4), 27-31.

Hutchins, C. L. (1994). State systems of education and systemic change. In C. M. Reigeluth & R. J. Garfinkle (Eds.), *Systemic change in education* (pp. 15-26). Englewood Cliffs, NJ: Educational Technology Publications.

Hunter, M. (1982). *Mastery teaching.* El Segundo, CA: TIP Publications.

Janesick, V. J. (1994). The dance of qualitative research design. In N. K. Denzin & Y. S. Lincoln (Eds.), *Handbook of qualitative research* (pp. 209-219). Thousand Oaks, CA: Sage Publications.

Jenlink, P., & Carr, A. A. (1996). Conversation as a medium for change in education. *Educational Technology, 36* (1), 31-38.

Jenlink, P. M., Reigeluth, C. M., Carr, A. A., & Nelson, L. M. (1996). An expedition for change: Facilitating the systemic change process in school districts. *Techtrends, 41* (1), 21-30.

Kemmis, S. C. (1987). Critical reflection. In M. Wideen and I. Andrews (Eds.), *Staff development for school improvement: A focus on the teacher.* (pp. 73-91). New York: Falmer Press.

Kincheloe, J. L. (1991). *Teachers as researchers: Qualitative inquiry as a path to empowerment.* Philadelphia, PA: Falmer Press.

Kincheloe, J. L. (1993). *Toward a critical politics of teacher thinking: Mapping the postmodern.* Westport, CT: Bergin & Garvey.

Kincheloe, J. L. (1998). Critical research in science education. In B. Fraser & K. Tobin (Eds.), *International handbook of science education* (p. 20). Boston: Kluwer Academic Publishers.

Kincheloe, J. L. (Ed.). (1999). *The post-formal reader: Cognition and education.* New York: Garland Press.

Kincheloe, J. L., & McLaren, P. L. (1994). Rethinking critical theory and qualitative research. In N. K. Denzin & Y. S. Lincoln (Eds.), *Handbook of qualitative research* (pp. 138–157). Thousand Oaks, CA: Sage Publications.

Kincheloe, J. L., & Steinberg, S. R. (1996). A tentative description of post-formal thinking: The critical confrontation with cognitive theory. In P. Leistyna, A. Woodrum, & S. A. Sherblom (Eds.), *Breaking free: The transformative power of critical pedagogy* (pp. 167–198). Cambridge, MA: Harvard Educational Review.

Kincheloe, J. L., & Pinar, W. F. (eds.). (1991). *Curriculum as social psychoanalysis: The significance of place.* Albany, NY: State University of New York Press.

Kohlberg, L. (1981). *The philosophy of moral development.* San Francisco: Harper Row.

Kuhn, T. S. (1996). *The structure of scientific revolutions* (3rd Ed.). Chicago: University of Chicago Press.

Lather, P. (1986). Research as practice. *Harvard Educational Review, 56* (3), 257–270.

Lather, P. (1988). Feminist perspectives on empowering research methodologies. *Women's Studies International Forum, 11* (6), 569–581.

Lather, P. (1992). Critical frames in educational research: Feminist and post-structural perspectives. *Theory into Practice, 31* (2), 87–99.

Louden, W. (1992). Understanding reflection through collaborative action research. In A. Hargreaves & M. Fullan (Eds.), *Understanding teacher development* (pp. 178–215). New York: Teachers College Press.

Lyotard, J. (1993). The entry into postmodernity: Nietzsche as a turning point. In T. Docherty (Ed.), *Postmodernism: A reader* (pp. 47–50). New York: Columbia University Press.

Mackinnon, A., & Grunau, H. (1994). Teacher development through reflection, community, and discourse. In P. P. Grimmett & J. Neufeld (Eds.), *Teacher development and the struggle for authenticity* (pp. 165–190). New York: Teachers College Press.

Marshall, J. D., & Sears, J. T. (1990). An evolutionary and metaphorical journey into teaching and thinking about curriculum. In J. T. Sears & J. D. Marshall (Eds.), *Teaching and thinking about curriculum: Critical inquiries* (pp. 15–32). New York: Teachers College Press.

National Commission on Excellence in Education. (1983). *A nation at risk: The imperative for educational reform.* Washington, DC: U.S. Government Printing Office.

National Staff Development Council in Cooperation with National Association of Secondary School Principals. (1995). *Standards for Staff Development: High School Edition—1995.* Reston, VA: National Association of Secondary School Principals.

Noddings, N. (1992). *The challenge to care in schools.* New York: Teachers College Press.

Patton, M. Q. (1990). *Qualitative evaluation and research methods* (2nd Ed.). Thousand Oaks, CA: Sage Publications.

Peat, F. D. (1991). *The philosopher's stone: Chaos, synchronicity, and the hidden order of the world.* New York: Bantam Books.

Peck, K. L., & Carr, A. A. (1997). Restoring public confidence in schools through systems thinking. *International Journal of Educational Reform, 6* (3), pp. 1–8.

Pinar, W. F. (1994). *Autobiography, politics and sexuality: Essays in curriculum theory 1972–1992.* New York: Peter Lang.

Pinar, W., Reynolds, W., Slattery, P., & Taubman, P. (1995). *Understanding curriculum.* New York: Peter Lang.

Polkinghorne, D. E. (1988). *Narrative knowing and the human sciences.* Albany: State University of New York.

Richardson, L. (1997). *Fields of play: Constructing an academic life.* New Brunswick, NJ: Rutgers University Press.

Rosenau, P. M. (1992). *Post-modernism and the social sciences: Insights, inroads, and intrusions.* Princeton, NJ: Princeton University Press.

Sarason, S. B. (1990). *The predictable failure of educational reform.* San Francisco: Jossey-Bass.

Schön, D. (1987). *Educating the reflective practitioner.* San Francisco: Jossey-Bass.

Schwandt, T. A. (1994). Constructivist, interpretivist approaches to human inquiry. In N. K. Denzin & Y. S. Lincoln (Eds.), *Handbook of qualitative research* (pp. 118–137). Thousand Oaks, CA: Sage Publications.

Senge, P. M. (1990). *The fifth discipline: The art and practice of the learning organization.* New York: Doubleday/Currency.

Sergiovanni, T. J. (1992). *Moral leadership: Getting to the heart of school reform.* San Francisco: Jossey-Bass.

Sergiovanni, T. J. (1994). *Building community in schools.* San Francisco: Jossey-Bass.

Sergiovanni, T. J., & Starratt, R. J. (1998). *Supervision: A redefinition* (6th Ed.). San Francisco: Jossey-Bass.

Shedd, J. B., & Bacharach, S. B. (1991). *Tangled hierarchies: Teachers as professionals and the management of schools.* San Francisco: Jossey-Bass.

Slattery, P. (1995). *Curriculum development in the postmodern era.* New York: Garland.

Smith, F. (1995). Let's declare education a disaster and get on with our lives. *Phi Delta Kappan, 76* (8), 584–590.

Spradley, J. P. (1979). *The ethnographic interview.* New York: Harcourt Brace Jovanovich College Publishers.

Steinberg, S. R., & Kincheloe, J. L. (Eds.). (1997). *Kinderculture: The corporate construction of childhood.* Boulder, CO: Westview Press.

Suarez, R. T. (1998). An inquiry into the historical meaning of "The Fifth Discipline." *Systemic Practice and Action Research, 11* (5), 483–502.

Sykes, G. (1996). Reform *of* and *as* professional development. *Phi Delta Kappan, 77* (7), 465–467.

Tanner, D., & Tanner, L. (1990). *History of the school curriculum.* New York: Macmillan.

Wagner, T. (1994). *How schools change: Lessons from three communities*. Boston: Beacon Press.

Wagschal, P. H. (1994 March). Hey Bucky, can you spare a paradigm? Reflections on synergetic education. *Bulletin: The National Association of Secondary School Principals,* 51–61.

Wilson, S., Peterson, P., Ball, D., & Cohen, D. (1996). Learning by all. *Phi Delta Kappan, 77* (7), 468–476.

Appendix A

Debriefing

One of the techniques that is supposed to enhance the accuracy or trustworthiness of what I report is called member checking. The way it works is that I give you the opportunity to critique what I write that relates to what you may have said, what you may have inferred, or my interpretation of what I think you said. The following are things to which I would like you to react. If you prefer to write a response, tape record a response, or meet and tell me your response, any of these is okay with me.

1. First, in my report I should be using pseudonyms for each of you. What name would you prefer to be called?
2. Initially I told you that any information that I had (such as my research proposal, books, and so on) you could use. I make note of this:

    Ironically, the participants made no requests for this information. At one point Sue expressed a desire to learn more about the effects of postmodernism on education, and I responded by providing her with Andy Hargreaves' book (1994). Besides this, the participants did not request any other information. My speculation is that this lack of interest was a reflection of their distrust of theory. I sensed that they valued the interaction of their own interpretations more than any theory that I could provide. The affective component of their remembrances undoubtedly reinforced the veracity of these memories and the new meanings constructed by this analysis of their past and present experience. Often the inability of theory to invoke emotion is to the detriment of the believability of the theory.

The documentation that I could provide was not forced on the participants because, in addition to the belief in the decision-making capabilities of the participants, Post-formal inquiry recognizes the value of the participants' indigenous knowledge and the participants' ability to create more complex cognitive structures from a critical examination of that knowledge.

My questions are as follows: Why didn't you request theoretical information? How accurate is what I wrote about your reasons for not requesting additional information?

3. The feedback papers that I gave to you after an interview contained questions from me to you about what you said, or as a way to expand the idea that was discussed.
   a. How effective were these questions in expanding the conversation?
   b. Did you actually think about them?
   c. What are your feelings about the value of the feedback papers and the technique of using questions in them to expand the conversation?
4. Was the theory included in the feedback papers valuable? Did it help you expand your awareness of the particular issue? What are your thoughts about interjecting theory into a professional development situation like I did?
5. One part of my report deals with affect or emotions as an important factor in the success and failure of educational change.
   a. What emotions did you experience at various times throughout the conversation that we had?
   b. Are the emotions that you experience at this point in your career similar to or different from the emotions that you experienced at other times in your career?
6. There is an attached paper entitled "Spiritual Crisis."
   a. What do you think of these ideas?
   b. How accurate are my interpretations about our experience at Cocalico in relation to this topic?
   c. How accurate is the last paragraph?
7. Would you estimate the amount of time that you spent working with the transcripts and the feedback papers.
8. What were the issues that were the most important to you that were generated by our conversations? Why were they so important?
9. Should conversation of this type be part of our professional development experience? Why?

Appendix B

Ray's Reflections on Barry's Interview
10/13—Session One

The following comments are my reflections on this interview. To facilitate an understanding of what I mean, if I use a technical word, I will provide a definition or explanation of the word or idea. If you wish to read more about the idea, I can provide more information. Also, for convenience I will bold the technical/theory words.

1. Overall I felt that your reflections dealt with school culture, community, and conversation. As for school culture, Andy Hargreaves talks about **balkanized**—in which groups of teachers are isolated from one another (by curriculum departments or by age); **collaborative and collegial**—where working relationships between teachers tend to be spontaneous, voluntary, focused on developing initiatives of their own, meetings aren't fixed in time but occur when the teachers decide they should occur, and the outcomes of this collegiality are unpredictable; **contrived collegiality**—relationships are administratively regulated, not spontaneous, meetings are compulsory, the focus is on implementing the mandates of others, the encounters take place at particular times and places as determined by the administration, and the outcomes are predictable due to the control of the administration; and **individualism**—in which teachers work in isolation due to constraints placed on them by administration or other constraints like the type of building or the type of school schedule, the fact that time cannot be wasted due to the amount of work that teachers have, or the fact that some teachers prefer to work alone. I see elements of all of these in your reflections.

2. Your description of the community or school system seems to be that of a top-down, hierarchical system with power centralized in the hands of the administration. Is this a correct reflection of your thoughts? Your comment that "we're not equals anymore. It's them and us, and they've created that them and us feeling" (p. 1) suggests a separation of administration and teachers and an adversarial relationship. Is this how it now is? You also said that "it used to be that because I was a professional we were equals"—does this mean that the system was more collegial or egalitarian in years past? If so, when and why? Also, why did it change? Which do you prefer? Using Hargreaves's cultures, how would you describe the current culture of Cocalico?

3. On pages one and two you talk about the difference between young and old teachers. Do you think that this is an example of Hargreaves's balkanization of teacher culture? How and why did the system change from the way you described it when you were a young teacher to now [the way it is]? Is this bad? If so, how could the system be changed? Would you prefer a collegial relationship with the younger teachers?

4. On pages three and four you talk about what I see as community. You talk of social and personal relationships between teachers (faculty parties, dinners, "sharing professional and personal experiences," and so on). How would you describe our community as of now? Why did the type of community change to what we have today? How would you reestablish the earlier community that you described? What would be your ideal school community? What would be the role of administration and students in this community?

5. At the top of page four you mention the open-space environment that we used to have. Was that a significant change from what we had prior to the open space and after the open space? Was our culture and our sense of community different before, during, and after open space? How so? Which would you prefer?

6. On page four you talk about football practice, social events, between-class conversations between teachers. It struck me that now those are not part of your professional life by your own choosing. Why? If you were more involved, would the isolation and perceived lack of respect from younger teachers be less? Why don't you socialize more with the faculty?

7. On page five you said that "I enjoy my autonomy in my classroom . . .". How much power do you have in your classroom? How much power do you have in relation to the school system? Why do you?
8. You said that we are always in the wrong place at the wrong time. Could you give an example? Why does this happen?
9. I am interested in the type of conversation that goes on in schools. These are types of conversation: (1) **Dialectical**—which is characterized by two adversarial sides that use logical arguments to win the discussion. In schools this is usually represented as administrators and experts/consultants on one side and teachers on the other. Since the administration/consultants/experts usually have access to all of the "knowledge/research," they usually win the conversation; (2) **Discussion**—the same as dialectical except since both parties don't "know" a lot, the conversation is more emotional and just as adversarial; (3) **Dialogue**—generally where the participants in the discussion put aside their preconceived mindsets and talk collegially to arrive at the best resolution of the problem. Here there is no adversality, but a common desire to do what is best to achieve the common vision or goal; (4) **Design**—which is like dialogue except it is concerned with changing the current system to better accommodate whatever change is intended. In design conversation you first develop a common vision and engage the system as an integrated whole instead of a collection of isolated parts. Design conversation always believes that any change in any single part of the system will affect the whole system.

    Okay, my questions are as follows: which of these types of conversation have you encountered during your career, and which have you not encountered? What were the conditions at the time that may have caused that type of conversation? Which to you is (are) the ideal type(s) of conversation? Which are harmful to a school community? Which help or hurt change attempts?
10. When we had the first interview you seemed emotional at times. How would you describe your feelings during the first interview?
11. What are your feelings about the conversations that you and I are having?

Appendix C

Feedback Paper after the First Group Conversation

TO: My conversation group
FROM: Ray Horn
DATE: 2/12/98
RE: Issues from the first group discussion

Thanks again for your time and sincere commentary. Despite the fiasco of the shredded tape, my backup system worked and I have our conversation on tape. Since it will take a while to get the tape transcribed, I would like to clarify a few issues that came up and [a few that] didn't come up but could have. Since Barry's neck problem will keep him from being in school, would it be possible to put your comments and decisions in some kind of written form and circulate them to all members of the group?

1. After the tape broke, the discussion about who determines faculty in-service program continued, and led into the possibility of our group formulating recommendations on faculty in-service program and presenting them to the administration. Sue's position was that the administration would be glad of input, and Barry's position was that they would be threatened by our input. Comments were also made about the outcomes from Barry's and my involvement in the CEA, [Cocalico Education Association] and that they have been somewhat significant and unexpected. The implication is that it is difficult to predict what will be the outcomes of teacher involvement in educational issues that arise in our school. The question is, do we want to pursue this by developing our conversation from its current form and function, to something related to what we were discussing? If so other questions would be as follows:

a. Would our purpose include developing a conversation with other teachers (especially less experienced ones), pursuing the in-service recommendations idea, and involving ourselves in other issues that traditionally have been in the purview of the administration?
b. Who would be included in our conversations?
c. Would our group become more formalized in its form and function?
d. What is our vision?
e. How can we sustain our group (find time to keep it going)?
f. How can we make this a fun thing as well as being professionally relevant?
g. Concerning Steve's idea that education is about asking questions, what other questions should we raise?

I am interested in your response to this idea and in the additional questions that you might raise.
2. Last night I related the story about knowing exactly what Sue was thinking when she asked the in-service question at the faculty meeting. Perhaps my intuitive understanding of her meaning was an unintended consequence of our dialogic discussions. Maybe when people engage in this kind of conversation they don't necessarily become like-minded but gain a better understanding of the other people. Also, I was sincere when I related my feelings about looking across the room at the more experienced teachers (during Sue's question and the principal's response), and thinking that these are the people who should be leading the decision making that affects our workplace. What is your feeling about this? Should we be the leaders?
3. Another issue that I didn't get to raise last night was a blurb from the faculty planning minutes for 2/4/98. "Hopefully the consistent five minutes in the revised schedules will help. The administration believes *that teachers must have ownership in the problem* to help relieve it." I became angry when I read this because I felt that it's a very disingenuous way of manipulating us. I immediately recalled the administration's rejection of our proposal for the faculty to become part of the management of discipline and the implementation of the new dress policy. I then recalled the manner in which the principal spoke *at* us about the failure of their discipline plan and the screw up concerning the duplicating paper. In each case, it was suggested that we were the cause of the problems, and it was done in a condescending manner—much like a parent to a child. Perhaps I'm just getting a bit hostile as my career winds down and senility sets in. However,

would it be appropriate for a group such as ours to create a dialogue about events such as these? Could we change things for the better by creating conversational opportunities for others concerning issues that are relevant and authentic to us?

4. In systems thinking, a man named Bertalanffy theorized that in systems there are "leading parts," or that in a system the more parts are specialized in a certain way, the more they are irreplaceable; and that the loss of parts may lead to the breakdown of the total system. I always saw Barry (the first assistant superintendent) as a leading part in the early reform efforts at Cocalico, and he was so important because he was able to empower others and form coalitions of others that enabled significant change to occur. He was a trigger that stimulated change in our system as much as Fran [a former assistant superintendent] was a trigger that marshaled the forces to stop the change initiatives of the 1970s. I propose that many of the experienced teachers are real leading parts in that if we didn't do what we do, things wouldn't get done. Therefore, do we have a responsibility to use our experience and power to form coalitions that will strive for better and more relevant education at Cocalico?

5. Finally, another idea from systems thinking is the idea of finality, in which the present is affected by the perception of the final state that will be reached. In education this would mean that change efforts are affected not only by the conditions of their implementation, but also by the individual or collective interpretation of the *perceived future*. For example, if portfolio assessment is being implemented and teachers are following a commercially prepared formula, the fact could be that significant implementation progress appears to be happening. However, if the teachers' vision of the future is that this is a fad that will not help them in the classroom and will pass away like all fads, then the teachers will be less committed, which will doom the long-term efficacy of the change. *Their interpretation* of the future affects the outcome of the change. During our discussion we were continually gloomy about the prospects of things getting better. Could this be because of our projected pessimism that is based on our current lack of empowerment or motivation? If we were actively involved in policy decisions at Cocalico, would the future appear so gloomy?

* If you have opinions about any of this, why not write them out and circulate them to us all.

Appendix D

**Ray's Reflections on Barry's Interview
11/14 —Session Two**

The following comments are my reflections on this interview. To facilitate an understanding of what I mean: if I use a technical word, I will provide a definition or explanation of the word or idea. If you wish to read more about the idea, I can provide more information. Also, for convenience I will bold the technical/theory words.

1. The central ideas or values that seemed to pervade this interview were collegiality, respect, ownership, conversation, and community.
2. Once again you appeared to make a distinction between our school of the '70s and our school of the more recent years. The former being more collegial in that there seemed to be more respect between everyone (including administration), that there was more faculty ownership in decision making, more dialogical conversation, and a sense of community. The last being marked by more balkanized and individualized relationships and a definite adversarial relationship between faculty and administration.
3. Overall, you describe education during your 30 years as cyclic, trendy, faddish, and bandwagonish.
4. When asked about power and decision making, you indicated that joint agreement—cooperation—is the best way.
5. Once again you mentioned the open space as a type of facility that allowed people to communicate freely. Since we are now in separate, self-contained classrooms governed by a block schedule, what could we do to promote the collegial conversation that you describe in relation to the "old days"? What lessons can we draw from the pre-open space and open-space days that can help us reestablish collegial conversation?

6. At one point I asked how you would change the school culture, and you replied that "I'm not sure that can be done." Later you saw a "tinge of hope" because of your meetings with the superintendent. Then you concluded that your relationship with Joe and Sharon is improved "because we've worked together . . . shared ideas together . . . learned that we are coming from some reasonable degree of common ground." You then identified dialogue as a key to achieving a "common goal . . . common agreement." You later said that "the motivation isn't there anymore. It would take somebody's effort to bring back that motivation" (p. 21). My question, which you started to answer in this interview, is, how can we start the process of creating a conversational community? You anticipated my question by this comment in the 11/14 interview:

> We've become more insightful in things. We see things we didn't see before. Maybe if true conversation were to take place, what needs to happen is to expand this group? Maybe it needs to start with a small group and then you add people and you add people and all of a sudden a similar situation to the 1970s does exist. Maybe that's what needs to occur. Maybe if we can include Sharon and Joe in the group maybe then they can bring somebody else in and that person brings somebody else in; and, maybe over time, given enough time, that group can expand into the type of group like we had before. Maybe that's one way to do it.

Also, you said that you and Dave expressed an interest in reading other people's comments, and the possibility of a roundtable activity. How would you recommend we go about this? Also, how would we evaluate the effectiveness of this sharing and conversation? What should we expect to happen or to see, if we are successful in our community-building efforts?

Appendix E

The Changing Organizational Culture

The Old Story	The New Story
Fixed, bureaucratic structure	Flexible, dynamic structure
Status-laden and rigid	Functional and evolutionary
Power resides at top	Power is shared by empowerment
Motivate, manipulate people	Inspire, care for each other
Compliance is valued	Creative contribution is valued
Focus on problems	Focus on opportunities
Blame people for failure	Encourage learning from failure
Short-term focus	Long-term perspective
Past regimen reinforced	Innovation and novelty nurtured
Work within constraints	Seek the ideal
Progress by increments	Progress by leaps
Technology and capital based	People and knowledge based
Linear/logical/reductionist	Dynamic/intuitive/expanding
Insisting on "the right way"	Encouraging learning/exploring
Driven by survival needs	Driven by desire to develop, fulfill self
External acknowledgment needed	Acknowledgment comes from self
Adversarial and competitive	Cooperative and supportive

Index

A Nation At Risk, 16
Ackoff, R., 100–101
Administration, 4, 9, 15–18, 59–60, 63, 67, 74–75, 80–82, 90–94, 97, 105, 109, 120–121, 131, 137, 140, 143, 146, 150, 159, 174, 178
Affect Control Theory, 26, 89–94, 113–114, 132
Alexander, D. C., 85
Alienation, 155
Alter, J., 43
Anderson, G. 26, 153
Anticipatory accommodation, 25–26, 116
Appendixes
 A, 30–31, 33, 125, 171–172
 B, 31, 34–35, 173–175
 C, 31, 40, 177–179
 D, 31, 124, 181–182
 E, 131, 183
Apple, M., 99
Audit Trails, 26
Avers, D., 71, 86–87

Banathy, B. H., 72, 86, 105, 129, 131, 153, 154
Barry, 6, 31–33, 34–37, 39–40, 44, 49–52, 55, 57–58, 61–62, 65–66, 74, 81–82, 95–96, 105, 115–116, 119–122, 124–125, 127–128, 131–136, 150, 172, 177, 181

Benking, H., 84
Bennett, K. P., 109
Berkeley, B., 11
Bertalanffy, L. V., 106–107, 156, 179
Block Scheduling, 59, 77, 131, 137, 144, 147, 181
Bohm, D., 73–80, 82, 86, 89, 157–158
Branson, R. K., 43
Breed, W., 155
Buber, M., 62–63, 145, 151
Butchart, R. E., 99

Canady, R. L., 131
Caring paradigm, 158
Carr, A. A., 71–72, 97, 101–102
Catalytic Inquiry, 24
Checkland, P., 100, 129
Clandinin, D. J., x, 112
Classroom Management/discipline, 14, 98–100
Cocalico Education Association, 177
Cocalico School District, 9–10, 174
Collegial Collaboration, 28–29, 118
Collen, A., 87
Community, 62–63, 67, 157, 174
 see egalitarian community
 community building, 120
Connelly, F. M., x, 112
Constructivism, 23, 99
Conversation
 critical dialogue, 73
 design, 71–72, 86–89, 175

dialectical, 14, 53, 71, 75, 80, 82, 86, 88, 91, 116, 123, 175
dialogue, 7, 27, 63, 71–73, 76–83, 86, 105, 116, 123, 135, 175
discussion, 71, 75, 86, 91, 175
generative, 86, 88–89
observational dialogue, 72–73
post-formal, 5, 24, 65, 67, 69, 84–89, 109–110, 121–122, 128, 157
significance of, 70–71
strategic, 86, 88
types of, 71–72
Critical Pedagogy, 19
Critical Theory, 22–24
Cuban, L., 109
Culture
balkanized, 55–60, 63–64, 93, 109, 115, 123, 125, 130, 136, 143, 152–153, 173–174, 181
collaboration, 55–56, 173
collegial, 65, 67, 173
contrived collegiality, 55–56, 130, 173
educational, 22
individualism, 55–60, 64, 93, 109, 115, 130, 136, 143, 152, 173, 181
organizational, 183
popular, 60–61
student, 60–61
teacher, 26, 55–60, 63
Currere, 26, 85
Curriculum and Instruction, 131, 151
collaborative groups, 16
continuous progress, 16
cooperative learning, 45
critical thinking, 45
flexible scheduling, 9
heterogeneous grouping, 11
individualized team teaching, 10, 11
instructional planning centers, 58, 136
mastery learning, 16
mini-courses, 10, 16
parallel disciplinary, 10–11

self-contained classrooms, 17, 58, 93, 125, 136, 181
small-group, 11, 16
technology, 103
teacher-centered/directed, 9, 15–17, 109

Dan, 6, 32, 34, 37, 40, 54–55, 58–59, 74, 98, 103, 115, 119, 125–127, 135, 150–152
Data Collection, 30
Dave, 6, 33, 36, 44–45, 61, 95, 97, 113, 115, 119–120, 124, 125, 127, 138–142, 146, 182
Debriefing, 124–125, 171–172
Dolbec, A., 87
Doll, W., 84

Educational Change
failure of educational change, 9
cyclic nature, 44
resistance to, 14
Educational Reform, 43–44
Egalitarian Community, 5, 89, 94–98, 159
Elkind, D., 47
Ellsworth, E., 32, 87
English Department, 10–11, 14–15, 37, 58, 133
Explicate order, 157
Ethnography, 22, 27
critical, 19, 24, 26–27, 115
critical constructivist, 23, 27, 113–115
descriptive, 23–24
interpretivist, 113–115
postmodern, 24
resistance-postmodernism, 27
Expertism, 52

Faules, D. F., 85
Feedback Papers, 28, 34–36, 114, 119, 123–124, 172
Flynn, E., 11
Fontana, A., 24, 29
Fourth Generation Evaluation, 22

Index

Freire, P. 27, 29, 34, 87
Frey, J. H., 24

Gender, 115, 120
Gilligan, C., 158
Giroux, H., 60, 97–98, 158
Grapes of Wrath, 11
Greene, M., 22
Gribbin, J., 70
Guba, E., 22–23
Gusky, T. R., 52

Habermas, J., 73, 79
Hargreaves, A., 32, 47, 55–56, 79, 109, 171, 174
High School Geography Project, 10
Horn, R. A., 112
Huberman, M., 52
Hunter, M., 45, 131
Hutchins, C. L., 104

Implicate order, 157–158
Inactive orientation, 154
Inquiry
  catalytic, 118
  design, 87
  emancipatory, 25–27
  moral, 99
  post-formal, 21–22, 24–25, 38, 115, 128–129
I-It relationship, 62–63, 119, 136, 146
Institutionalizing of Education, 108–110
Interactive orientation, 154
Interviewing, 29–30
Introduction to the Social Studies, 10, 14–15, 59
I-Thou relationship, 62–64, 119, 141, 146, 152

Janesick, V., 26
Jenlink, P. M., 71–72, 102
Journals, 30–32, 114

Kincheloe, J. L., 22–26, 53, 60, 84–85, 112, 117, 157
Kohlberg, 158

Kuhn, T., 69

Landscape, 112
Lather, P. 24, 26–27, 53
Learning Organizations, 64–66
LeCompte, M., 109
Lincoln, Y., 22–23
Loose Coupling, 109
Louden, W., 72–73
Lyotard, J., 52

Macedo, D. P., 27, 34, 87
Marshall, J. D., 95
Marx Brothers, 11
Master Teacher, 13, 16, 107
McEwan, B., 99
McLaren, P., 22–24, 117
Megaskills, 45
Member Checking, 26, 124–125
Middle States Evaluation, 16
Minton, E., 45
Modernism, 21, 48–49, 60, 70, 110, 126–127, 129, 157
Moral Commitment, 57

Narrative
  autobiographical, 111
  biographical, 111
  collective story, 111
  critical moments, 111–112
  cultural, 111
  everyday narrative, 111
  landscape, 112
  post-formal story, 111–112

National Commission on Excellence, 16
Noddings, N., 158

Open Space
  Classroom, 12, 15–16, 92
  facility, 12, 15, 94
  initiative, 15, 74–75
  school, 144
Organizational Culture, 183
Outcome-based Education, 17–18, 107

Patton, M. Q., 26, 29
Peat, F., 157
Peck, K., 101–102
Pinar, W. 26, 41, 53, 85
Polkinghorne, D. E., 111–112
Popular Culture, 60
Portfolio Assessment, 17, 44–46, 54, 75, 96–97, 179
Post-formalism, 19, 154
    conversation, 5, 24, 65, 67, 69, 84–89, 94, 109–110, 121–122, 128, 157
    inquiry, 21–22, 24–25, 27–28, 38, 42, 113, 172
    research, 27
    skills, 5
    stories, 111–112
    thinking, 84–87, 97
Postmodernism, x, 6, 19, 21, 32, 46–47, 53, 55, 62, 67, 110
    see resistance postmodernism
Power, 21–23, 26–27, 56, 74, 85, 94, 94–97, 107, 109, 115–116, 120, 122
    see student power
Praxis, 27, 34, 65, 158
Preactive orientation, 154
Professional Development, x, 5, 18, 141
    modernistic, 48–49
    post-formal, 126–128, 156
    reconceptualization, 88
Psychoanalytic Analysis of Place, 26

Race, 115, 120
Ray, 34, 39, 51–52, 57–59, 65, 81–82, 92–93, 97–98, 119, 142, 144, 146, 150–152, 173, 177, 181
Reactive orientation, 153
Reflection
    autobiographical reflection, 4, 54–55
    critical reflection, x, 7, 21, 26, 111
Researchers, 23
    as participant, 28
    post-formal, 27

praxis-oriented, 25
Resistance Postmodernism, 117–118
Richardson, L., 111
Roosevelt, F., 11
Root Definition, 129
    Modernistic, 129
    Post-formal, 130
Rosenau, P. M., 47
Roundtables, 83–84

Sarason, S., 94, 97
Scholes, 129
Schön, D., 72–73, 79
Schrödinger's Cat, 70
Schwandt, T. A., 23
Sears, J., 95
Semiotics, 19
Senge, P., 64–66, 73–74, 102
Sergiovanni, T., 64, 79
Shedd, J. B., 95
Slattery, P., 62
Smith, F., 43
Social construction of meaning, 104
Social Studies Department, 10–18, 145
Spiritual Crisis, 61–64, 128
Spirituality, x, 19, 151, 172
Spradley, J. P., 22–23, 26
Steve, 6, 33, 35, 37, 49–51, 55, 74, 115, 119–120, 124–125, 127, 135, 142–149, 178
Steinbeck, J., 11
Steinberg, S. R., 60, 85, 157
Student Empowerment, 97–99, 120
Sue, 6, 32–33, 35, 39–41, 44, 47–48, 58, 60–61, 65–66, 74, 82, 91–93, 98, 113–115, 118, 120, 124–125, 136–138, 141, 171, 177–178
Standards For Staff Development: High School Edition:1995, 95
Student Culture, 60–61
Suarez, R. T., 65–66
Sykes, G., 53
Symbolic Interactionism, 19, 74
Synergy, 28, 38
Systemic Fault, 75

Systemic Illiteracy, 105
Systemic View, 100, 105
Systems Theory, x, 6, 19, 100
Systems Thinking, 26, 89, 100–101, 116
    boundaries, 100, 104–105
    finality, 100, 107–108
    imperviability and leverage, 101–104, 153
    leading parts, 100, 106–107
    progressive segregation, 100, 106

Tanner, D., 109
Tanner, L., 109
Teachers, 159
    as systemic agents of change, 100
    empowerment of, 94–97
    Inclusion in policy making, 42
    knowledge, x
    moral commitment, 57
    self-esteem, 90–91
    teacher-as-gatekeeper, 6
    teacher-as-person, 6

Teacher Culture, 26, 116
    balkanized, 55–60, 63–64, 93, 109, 115, 123, 125, 130, 136, 143, 152–153, 173–174, 181
    collaboration, 55–56
    collaborative, 63, 173
    collegial, 65, 67, 173
    contrived collegiality, 55–57, 130, 173
    individualism, 55–60, 64, 93, 109, 115, 130, 136, 143, 152, 173, 181
Transformative Intellectual, 158
Triangulation, 26
Trustworthiness, 25–27, 115–117

Validity, 26–27
    catalytic, 25
Vision, 64–66, 105, 135

Wagner, T., 46
Wagschal, P. H., 69
Wilson, S., 48

Studies in the Postmodern Theory of Education

General Editors
Joe L. Kincheloe & Shirley R. Steinberg

Counterpoints publishes the most compelling and imaginative books being written in education today. Grounded on the theoretical advances in criticism, feminism, and postmodernism in the last two decades of the twentieth century, Counterpoints engages the meaning of these innovations in various forms of educational expression. Committed to the proposition that theoretical literature should be accessible to a variety of audiences, the series insists that its authors avoid esoteric and jargonistic languages that transform educational scholarship into an elite discourse for the initiated. Scholarly work matters only to the degree it affects consciousness and practice at multiple sites. Counterpoints' editorial policy is based on these principles and the ability of scholars to break new ground, to open new conversations, to go where educators have never gone before.

For additional information about this series or for the submission of manuscripts, please contact:
      Joe L. Kincheloe & Shirley R. Steinberg
      c/o Peter Lang Publishing, Inc.
      275 Seventh Avenue, 28th floor
      New York, New York 10001

To order other books in this series, please contact our Customer Service Department:
      (800) 770-LANG (within the U.S.)
      (212) 647-7706 (outside the U.S.)
      (212) 647-7707 FAX

Or browse online by series:
      www.peterlang.com